# Sigh

We Inhale Obstacles &
We Exhale a Life of Love

# Sigh

## Lesley Marcovich
on behalf of All of Us

ISBN (paperback): 978-1-0690675-0-0
ISBN (ebook): ISBN 978-1-0690675-1-7

Book design and production by www.AuthorSuccess.com

Printed in the United States of America

Because we are all an authority
on the subject matter in this book,
it is therefore dedicated to All of Us.
SIGH salutes YOU!

\*A detailed list of all topics discussed herein
is chronicled at the back of the book

# SIGH

True love means taking from others
as we reach over and remove obstacles
from their paths.

*L* et
*O* thers
*V* enture
*E* asily

In this book we do not discredit each other, we do not
criticize each other, and we do not tell each other how we
should be, or how we should journey through life.

*Why?* Because this book is a celebration of who we all
truly are, deep down at our core: a very special celebration
that shines a radiant light on how we remove obstacles from
each other's paths, and how we get out of each other's way,
whilst travelling courageously and confidently through time.
In other words, how we express the deepest meaning of the
most powerful, all-encompassing word – LOVE.

This book is a crystal-clear reflection of **ALL OF US**.

# INTRODUCTION

*Some of Jamie's first memories are of Mum and Dad look-ing worried and sad, then Mum rubbing her eyes and Dad leaving the room, and then afterwards they are very quiet when they eat dinner. This happens many times over the years, and this is when a small, powerless child is able to help.*

*There is no television in the country where Jamie grows up; instead, radio is the link to the world, along with the entertainment. Jamie loves cuddling up between his parents in their bed, where they listen to great comedies, quiz shows, and dramas, while they laugh and cheer and shriek with fear.*

*After the 'quiet' dinnertimes Jamie runs into the main bedroom, jumps onto his parents' bed, and shouts, "Mummy, Daddy, The Colonel's Courtroom is starting in six minutes!" Then, after his parents edge their way un-der the covers to lay beside him, Jamie takes their hands, and slowly, throughout the show, he eases them closer towards each other, until they touch.*

*Jamie believes that this is where his expression of love begins; as a powerless, innocent child, not able to 'do' something for others during their time of need, but rather to take something away from them, namely some of their stress, even if it is only for half an hour.*

*Jamie does not believe that he is an overly demon-strative person now in his later years – quick to hug, say "I love you" and plaster all his loving thoughts on social media – but he DOES love. He loves by finding every opportunity to not add stress to others, and also to relieve others of stress, and pain, whenever and wherever he can.*

## *Our Love Is the Breath of Life*

TO BEGIN, WE BREATHE IN. As we inhale, we draw others into our hearts, accepting them for who they are and where they are headed, and if we notice any debris within their lives, we gracefully reach over and pull it from their path.

AND THEN, WE BREATHE OUT. As we exhale, we become a part of others' hearts, surrendering our own feelings and expressing our love, through well-wishing words and affectionate gestures.

On our road of life, we move. We stop. We take from others. We move. We stop. Others take from us. On and on we travel . . . moving, stopping, taking, moving, stopping, giving thanks, moving, stopping, taking . . .

> Our loving breath
> – a long, deep SIGH –
> is our formula for living
> as we all breathe together
> in perfect synchronicity
> of taking and giving
> . . . in . . . out . . . in . . . out . . .
>
> *All of Us*

## *There May Be Times When Our Breath Is Constricted*

There may be times when we are unable to help others because of a decline in the health of our body, or our mind, or our psyche/subconscious/inner-self/soul (however we view the driving force in our life) and this condition can cast a variety of obstacles onto our path: grief, stress, shame, defiance, doubt, helplessness, hate, fear, ferocity, pain, paralysis, alienation, etc.

But then, being the beautiful, loving beings which we all are, it is not long before our obstacles are graciously removed by others, and we are able to continue on our journey, and then thankfully do the same for others during a decline in their health.

Everyone is constantly reaching out in each direction
– this side, that side – moving debris, clearing ways.
Everyone is constantly breathing in chorus together
– in to our hearts, out to others' hearts –
every moment of our days.

## *Our Love Rides On a Wonderous, High-Frequency Wave*

Our universe is made up of powerful energy, vibrating at various frequency levels, that we feel all around us as we stroll through a lush, green forest, or as we congregate in a room of people whose emotions are focused on love.

The frequency of love is at the same level as many miraculous things all around us; like rainbow colours and the buzz of queen bees, and it is also at the same level where peace, joy, and strength exist. As we vibrate at these high frequencies, things become clearer to us, which gives us the focus to help others rise to a high level as well.

We all ride on an infinite, high-frequency wave
that moves sands of time onto our shore
lifting us and thrusting us towards the light,
where we rest, we rejoice, and we restore.

# WHO WE ALL ARE

We are multi-layered, mighty beings, equipped with re-markable tools, which advance us on our journey through life, and unite us all in true love.

## *We Embrace Each Other's Uniqueness*

We are all unique, like snowflakes, which all have the same symmetry when they are formed. However, as they drift down, they are buffeted by winds, humidity, pollu-tion, temperature fluctuations, and many other variables, which cause complex structural changes to their shapes; exactly the same thing that happens to us during our lives. This means that we all have different needs, at different times, of our ever-changing existence.

We accept and embrace the uniqueness in each other, ultimately sticking together to form a glittering, expansive, milky blanket on our world, which makes it a fascinating and illuminating place to live, and thrive.

## *Who We Are at Our Core*

'Who we are' is more than our personalities – our interests, ambitions, ingrained behaviours, emotional patterns, and how we adjust to life, etc. – it is the many layers of our common symmetry; the basic nature which we are all born with. We are:

◊ Our *valiant* ancestors – who faced famines, plagues, perilous journeys, and conflicts, with courage and honour – continue to flourish and glorify life inside of us, every single day.

◊ The *trusting* baby in us – who listens, gurgles, smiles, and squeals, as it welcomes all connectivity – continues to promote social interaction, every single day.

◊ The *playful* child in us – who wears enchanted hats and poses in a superhero stance, who hugs animals both big and small, who skips and cartwheels, and sings out loud – continues to laugh and engage, every single day.

◊ The *brave-hearted* teenager in us – who flaunts cool clothing, attitude, and creativity – continues to let loose and express, every single day.

◊ The *romantic* young adult in us – who reaches for the stars, in both love and in life – continues to aspire to new heights, every single day.

◊ The *nurturing* parent in us; to ALL Earth's children – whose arms are open wide to others – continues to nurture, mentor, and comfort, every single day.

◊ The *adventurous* traveller in us – whose lens is poised and whose heart is open to distant horizons – continues to explore and discover the world, every single day.

◊ The *sensational* artist in us – who conveys who we are in how we design, decorate, and perform, with a colourful spirit – continues to sweeten the world, every single day.

◊ The *dedicated* collector in us – who collects shoes, pictures, wisdom, and knowledge – continues to gather, maintain, and share all the treasures of the world, every single day.

◊ The *triumphant* winner in us – who wins a donut, a good debate, or a grand prize – continues to celebrate victories in many forms, every single day.

◊ The *innovative* achiever in us – who hosts a dinner party, cultivates a vegetable garden, or discovers a cure – continues to give birth to an idea and follows through on it, every single day.

◊ The *enthusiastic* joy-seeker in us – who lives life to the fullest, seeking pleasant thrills and fascination – continues to light up our life and inspire others, every single day.

◊ The *confident* dreamer in us – who soars on the wings of hope – continues to search for a rainbow, every single day.

◊ The *loving* friend in us – who offers a warm smile, a sympathetic ear, and a welcoming heart – continues to open new doors for others, every single day.

We are valiant, trusting, playful, brave-hearted, romantic, nurturing, adventurous, sensational, dedicated, triumphant, innovative, enthusiastic, confident, and loving.

We are VIBRANT BEINGS! Every one of us.
Every single day.

We are all EQUALLY significant on this planet. Like a small drop in the pond, the ripple effect of our existence has an enormous, widespread impact on family, friends, community, country, and the world. Our understanding, acceptance, and reverence of who we are enables us to understand, accept, revere, and sincerely love everyone and everything around us.

# OUR LIFE JOURNEY

*Sabrina, a teacher, mother, and writer, needs to stop for a moment to take inventory and re-evaluate her life, before making a major career change. She decides that it may be a good time to reflect on her life journey thus far, so she visualizes her funeral whilst she writes her own eulogy.*

*This is when Sabrina shines a bright light on her life up until this point: her achievements, her setbacks, her dreams, and the gratitude towards all those who have played, and continue to play an important role in her life.*

*Because this exercise is so profound for Sabrina, she decides to continually keep her eulogy updated, until one day, after several years, there is enough material about general life goals, love, and gratitude, for her to write a book, which gets published by the new company she begins working for when she changes her career.*

We have all faced a large number of obstacles of various shapes and sizes during our lives up until now, and when we look back we can see where we stepped out of our own way – alone, or with the help of others – and where we were able to get back onto our path again.

We are strong. We are resilient. We are all authors of great, award-winning memoirs. We are.

## *Our Journeys Are Unique*

We are all on our own personal journey – whether we believe that this life is our 'one and only' life, or whether we believe that this life is one of many lives within a higher spiritual realm – and we continually strive to fill our present life with purpose, meaning, and abundant happiness.

Our journeys are as unique as who we are; how we see things, how we comprehend things, and how we feel. By accepting how unique our journeys are, we gain an understanding of how challenging it can be to try to steer others onto different paths.

We are all our own mentors, at our own pace, in our own time, as we witness and experience things that we store in our mental files marked 'observations,' 'conclusions,' 'memories,' 'goals,' and so on. Everyone's private filing cabinet is one-of-a-kind, and if transcribed it is approximately the size of a small country.

We are all vibrant beings
taking paths which we choose
knowing that we're the only ones
who can walk in our shoes.

## *Life Isn't Always a Smooth Journey*

Here we are, travelling along our road of life, when suddenly we come upon a roadblock— an enormous, immovable rock that makes us slam on our brakes and screech to a stop! We raise our eyes to take in the full magnitude of the rock: its size, its hardness, its power, its dominance. Life will never be the same again.

After some time we blink, take our gaze off the rock, and survey the landscape – to the left, to the right – and then, with a shrug of our shoulders and a nod of our head, we veer off the road and scramble into the rough country . . .
No rock, no matter what size, is going to stop us.

Through the rough country we travel, losing our balance as we clamber over boulders, pulling out thorns as we fumble through thickets, shivering from cold as we wade through rivers and trudge through marshes . . .
No harsh terrain is going to stop us.

Onward we travel, grappling in every direction as we stagger through shadowy, dense forests, parting the trees, forging our path . . .
No darkness is going to stop us.

We keep going, and going, straining our vision through dense mist, seeking shelter through soaking rain, maintaining our steadiness through whipping wind, gritting our teeth under ground-shaking thunder . . .
No violent weather is going to stop us.

We keep our eyes focused ahead, our arms swaying, our feet moving . . . onward . . . onward . . . onward . . .

Days become weeks, or months, or sometimes years, and during this challenging period we grow stronger, smarter, and way more savvy.

Soon we begin to shout in the face of the terrain, the darkness, and the weather, as our breath deepens, our eyes brighten, our backs straighten, and our steps quicken.

## *We Are Not Alone in the Rough Country*

As we trudge wearily through the rough country, there are times when we hear the distant sound of people shouting; acknowledging us, comforting us, reassuring us, and cheering us on! This tells us that, come what may, we are never alone.

The uplifting sound of the voices motivates us to pull out and utilize all of our natural life tools; tools that help us to:

1. Shut out negatives and focus on positives.

2. Dress our wounds.

3. Implement new ways.

4. Navigate with skill.

5. Be aware of our surroundings and keep ourselves safe.

6. Pick up our pace.

7. Steady and balance our lives so that we stand in good stead for when the time comes for us to skip back onto our road.

*Pieter, who works in a juice-processing plant, says, "I think of the pieces of fruit I process as people." Here is how he describes juicing the apples:*

1. *They are freshly picked, standing on the assembly line, poised to be pressed into juice. (The pure essence of who they are.) We all stand by, ready to begin the process, aware that we don't always have the knowledge of outcomes.*

2. *We begin by cleansing the apples of harmful bacteria. (We help them to remove everything that is eating away at them.)*

3. *We shred the apples into a workable pulp, which is easier to press. (We break down their feelings by opening communication and awareness.)*

4. *And then we press, acquiring the pure, sweet nectar of the fruit. (We draw out the true essence of who they are, right down to their core.) The pulp is never wasted; instead, after the press, it is used to feed animals. (None of their experiences are ever wasted; instead they are used for knowledge and for the understanding of life's ordeals.)*

*During this process there are times when there's too much heat, or not enough heat involved, amongst many other setbacks. However, we continue to evaluate and try different approaches throughout the process, until good outcomes are achieved.*

Our lives are regularly interrupted by a broad range of obstacles; like the gridlock of insecurity, the delays of distress, the detours of mishaps, and the roadblocks of fear. These setbacks can redirect us to an alternative route of new perspectives and possibilities, where, often, with the pure love of others, we can skip back onto our road again, filled with optimism and confidence.

Some obstacles are checkpoints in our lives, where, after taking detours, we are able to learn, and change, and in some cases, grow.

We are always on standby – waiting, observing – ready to step in to do whatever we can, to help each other navigate the rough country with our goodness and grace, which is the golden nectar of who we all are.

## *We Don't Fall for Tricksters on Our Path*

Sometimes we come across tricksters (nagging thoughts) on our path, that try to confuse us with ideas of good and bad, should and shouldn't, with and against, etc., but we don't pay heed to these pesky little illusionists who can sometimes carry us off into the endless drama of a manipulative movie entitled "Who We Think We Are."

We shove tricksters off our own paths, and others' paths too, as we question many of our thoughts and turn them around to reveal their truths. This way we do not run off with any polarizing thoughts; but instead we settle down in front of a great, factual, unifying movie entitled "Who We Truly Are."

*"Grab the popcorn! Start the show!"* we triumphantly proclaim.

Our individual journeys of moving, stopping, taking, moving, stopping, and giving thanks, amount to a five-star, unified planet, produced and directed by All of Us.

# OUR BASIC HUMAN NEEDS

.

In order to survive, we require air, water, food, sleep, and shelter, and most importantly we require the neurological and psychological sense of 'belonging,' which safeguards our survival.

We are all born with a supreme, life-preserving 'belonging' circuitry, as the baby in us demonstrates by staring, smiling, fussing, crying, and cuddling, because we depend on the assurance that social attachments are near-at-hand, to protect us from hunger and danger.

Our connectivity is critical for our basic survival, and the fact that we have all been surviving for many millennia on our fruitful planet, shows that our baby mindset is the fundamental framework that keeps us moving and removing obstacles from each other's paths, so that we can all keep cohabitating through our comfortable, cuddly connections.

## We Do Not Banish Others from the Tribe

Our amygdala, one of the most primitive parts of our modern brain, is our threat detector. This great warning system is on constant alert for danger, and for any changes that occur in our lives. When we are faced with change, our brain hollers:

*"Alert! Alert! This is threatening and it demands a lot of mental energy."*
*"We need to keep life predictable and safe, in order to save power."*
*"The old 'you' is better."*
*"We must not change. Look at what it will do to us!"*

Our apprehension towards any changes in our lives results from not feeling confident enough to handle change. This is when we consider strategies to take away primal fears so that change can be managed and oftentimes, embraced, as we move forward down endless corridors, taking huge breaths and flinging open door after door after door.

When change is inevitable, we are all here for each other, offering reassurance that no matter what happens, nobody will be banished from the 'tribe.'

We greet one another with a welcoming smile
we express our needs together
we hold one another in a warm embrace
as the baby in us lives on, forever.

# OUR FOUR NATURAL LIFE TOOLS

We are all outfitted with Talents, Intuition, Morals, and Emotions, which is the power that drives us to become magnificent masters of our lives, as we maximize our greatest gift: TIME.

## 1. Our Talents

Like a birthmark, we are born with it. It is unique. It shows up at different times and places. It is our talent; a highly elevated form of communication, showing us, and others, what humans are capable of, and how brilliant we are at achieving remarkable things.

Our list of talents is endless: archery, soccer, listening, carpentry, bilingualism, healing, salesmanship, humour, knotting and knitting, and many, many more.

## We Embrace Our Talents

*Angelika says, "I am passionate about making jewellery – selecting from Earth's wonderful mineral supply and piecing it together in attractive displays that symbolize celebration and love – all this to enhance self-expression, and add style to the beautiful people I meet."*

We tap into our talents by releasing ourselves into a brilliant, creative realm, where we allow ourselves to be lost and to be found, to be led and to follow, and to float in a timeless sea of memories, awareness, passion, and vision.

Our talents sweeten the world by making it:
- more beautiful; through art, landscaping, and colourful decorations
- more spirited; through entertainment, games, and open communications
- more functional; through architecture, transportation, and medical innovations

## *We Cast Our Lines Far Out Into the Lake of Creativity*

- *When we go fishing, we begin by stringing our pole.*
  When we are creative, we begin by igniting the part of our brain that blocks out distractions and allows us to focus.
- *When we go fishing, after our pole is strung, we then bait our hook.*
  When we are creative, we then ignite the part of our brain that recalls the past and reshapes it into new ideas, theories, and possibilities.
- *When we go fishing, after our hook is baited, we then cast our line.*
  When we are creative, we then ignite the part of our brain that sorts through, and analyzes

all the information gathered, and then we illuminate our world with beauty, connections, and insight.

We all have the power to think taller, wider, and deeper, and we cast our line far, far, far, out into the Lake of Creativity, knowing that if we do not, we may miss the big fish.

Our world grows through our talents and achievements; therefore we are always ready to help each other untangle lines, find bait, and sweep rods forward, so that everyone's catch can feed, please, and preserve our powerful planet in countless ways.

Our talents are priceless gifts to both ourselves, and to others, who may be inspired by them to fulfill their dreams.

Our talents keep on giving
and this keeps us living
generation after generation
as we continue casting . . . casting . . .

## 2. Our Intuition

Our intuition inhabits the empty spaces within our body, especially the spaces within our heart. It is the reaction of the body – a tugging, an attraction, a warning – before our conscious mind comprehends what is happening, so that we instantly see, and feel, the big picture all at once.

As flocks of geese fly overhead, heading thousands of miles away in a perfect chevron-shaped flight formation, we know with certainty that there are trillions of unexplainable, wordless voices protecting and advancing our survival on Earth – an inherent, innate intelligence – the very same intelligence which intuition is a part of.

## We Keep Our Intuition Lines Wide Open

*"Do whatever your gut is telling you."*

*"If you have an uneasy feeling about this, then don't do it."*

*"If that's what you want deep down, then go for it."*

We trust each other's 'sometimes illogical' decisions – when brains flash back to past experiences and pick up current signals and cues – because we know that intuition is not all over the map; it is a steady, focused, committed feeling which takes us by the hand and leads us to where we want, or need, to be.

If our intuition becomes blocked at any point due to an overthinking, congested, overanalytical mind – where we have left too many tabs open – we go on an expedition within, to the gaps between our thoughts, to the control room of our consciousness, and we tap into the open spaces where our watchful guide, or sixth sense is housed.

Earth is one massive magnet, and as we journey on our road of life, our own personal compasses (intuitions) move freely, continually pointing us towards our true north, towards our natural, loving self, which enables us all to fly in a grand formation together.

Living a grand, loving life is something we 'intuitively' want and need, so we do it!

## 3. *Our Morals*

Our morals, housed within the largest parts of our brain, are our natural sense of beliefs and values about what is right and what is wrong; a sense which can change positively and productively over time, through personal experiences and outside influences.

*M* erciful
*O* pen-minded
*R* ighteous
*A* ltruistic
*L* oyal
*S* incere

When we make decisions during our lives, we understand that everyone views outcomes and futures through different lenses, and so, as we tap into our own personal morals, we accept and welcome others' viewpoints, which are based on their personal morals at the time.

If we believe in DESTINY, magic unfolds before us. We follow up on random experiences and people we encounter, we stop and ruminate before we act, and we accept that detours and challenges are guides on our journey towards our predetermined future.

If we are FREE-THINKERS, we believe that we are the agents over our own lives. We use logic, reasoning, and practical observations to make decisions, and we believe that the cards which life deals us are not responsible for the things that happen to us. WE are.

Merciful, open-minded, righteous, altruistic, loyal, and sincere, are all beautiful flowers stemming from one towering, universal plant called SHARING.

*There is a camera set up next to a small man-made watering hole in an African desert, where at one point a herd of antelope gather to drink, and once they leave, a team of buffalo gather to drink, and once they leave, a tower of giraffe gather to drink. And while all of this takes place, far off in the background one can see an occasional warthog darting back and forth, waiting for its turn to share in the life-giving liquid.*

'Sharing' blooms brilliantly, all year round
even in a dry, dusty, desert ground.

- When we are *M*erciful, we share our time and our energy, to relieve others of their suffering.
- When we are *O*pen-minded, we share our flexibility and ideas, to help others achieve good results.

- When we are *R*ighteous, we share our positive ideals, to set good standards for community living.
- When we are *A*ltruistic, we share the best interests of everyone, to spread goodwill to all living things.
- When we are *L*oyal, we share our devotion and trust, to support and expand noble causes.
- When we are *S*incere, we share our authenticity and transparency, to remind others of who they truly are.

Our morals create collective, life-giving standards that enable us to thrive happily together; as a family, as a community, and as a species, around all of Earth's wondrous, watering holes.

## 4. Our Emotions

Our emotions – the voices of our bodies, interconnected deep within our brain – drive us to take action in our need for survival. Most of our daily lives are driven by emotions that help us to avoid danger, while seeking happiness. Our emotions are essential for motivation, learning, decision-making, growth, and overall well-being, as we experience an event, react to it, and then respond to it.

There can be thousands of thoughts attached to just one emotion. If an emotion is a little troubling, as we process it by observing it, unravelling its origin, and then working hard to set it free, we clear the way in our brain for thousands of better, more productive thoughts to generate.

Emotions emit immensely powerful vibrations that keep us, and others, fully aware and fully alive. Emotions are, in essence, the stories beneath our stories.

Sympathy, gratitude, worry, and delight
we work with our emotions to do what feels right.

By recognizing, understanding, and cherishing all of our natural life tools, we are able to recognize, understand, and accept everyone else's natural life tools, as we all master the powerful experience of being alive.

## What Connects Us to Our Outer World?

Our four natural life tools would not be worth anything without the rational, decision-making, driving force which exists between our inner-being and our outer-world: the 'I'; i.e. the EGO. Ironically, our ego is located within the frontal portion of our brain, which is a good place to be located because it leads us through life. Our ego believes in our abilities, while it constantly drives us towards personal growth, higher aspirations, and excellence.

### Our Egos to the Rescue

Our egos mirror our self-confidence, self-determination, and self-reliability, especially when we come upon road-blocks. With our invincible sense of 'I' we leap forward, overcome obstacles, and in some cases we accept, and grow exponentially from their intrusion.

We are fully equipped to create personal standards, inspire others, and navigate towards greatness, with our own profound sense of aliveness and self-worth; our distinctly dotted **i**.

What amazing mortals we are; existing on a pristine planet, each gifted with a bountiful, bottomless bag of superb, sophisticated tools.

We are all in this together
right here, right now
knowing who we truly are.
We help others on their journey
with care and with love
so that we may all find ways
to travel afar.
*All of Us*

# WE TAKE FROM OTHERS AS WE ILLUMINATE THE WHOLE GLOBE WITH A RADIANT, PURE LIGHT OF LOVE

Our stories – who we are and how we journey through life – are the invisible strands that hold our DNA together, as we use our natural tools to form loving relationships with everyone and everything surrounding us.

## *What Are Our Relationships?*

Our relationships represent houses, the FOUR parts of a house that add up to, and model, pure love: the foundation, the walls, the roof, and the décor.

1. **THE FOUNDATION:** Respect is the mortar that keeps the foundation of our relationships solid and immovable; respect for each other's past, dreams, and life journey.

2. **THE WALLS:** Memories and experiences make up the walls, which aren't always straight or perfect. Some are flimsy, some are temporary, and some are solid. The walls are there to hold up our relationships and define the various stages of our

lives, which are forever changing; often working with us, sometimes working against us.

3. **THE ROOF:** The roof is the commitment piece of our relationships, built to withstand the fiercest of storms. No matter what, the roof remains secure; sheltering and protecting the entire relationship design.

4. **THE DÉCOR:** The décor consists of all the merriment, the games, and the shenanigans in our relationships, that keep us liking each other, that keep us human, and that keep our feet planted firmly on the ground.

Like anything built to withstand traffic, climate, and erosion, our relationship with every living thing on Earth requires constant inspection and maintenance, and sometimes when things get rickety or tired— a renovation, and sometimes when things literally crumble to the ground— a complete restoration.

There are times when we stop and ask ourselves:

- *"How is our house holding out?"*
- *"Do we need to fortify or build a firmer, or different foundation?"*
- *"Do we need to repair, refurbish, or move a few walls?"*
- *"Do we need to reinforce, realign, or construct a brand-new roof?"*
- *"Do we need to redecorate?"*

We inherently know that it is never too late to start modifying our respect, our experiences, our commitment, and our mood. After all, there is nothing better than the smell of freshly-poured concrete, new paint, flowing tar, and the powerful, intoxicating scent of life interactions.

We now enter our HOUSE, all united in a long, deep sigh, of pure, life-sustaining love.

*i*

# PART ONE

# THE FOUNDATION

Respect is the mortar that keeps the
foundation of our relationships
solid and immovable;
respect for each other's past, dreams, and life journey.

When Respect speaks, it says, *"I perceive you, I accept you, I feel your pain. I am here for you, I honour you, and together, forever, we will flourish."*

## *The Powerful Materials Used in the Foundation*

Our relationship foundations are all built using three potent, durable materials, each containing three ingredients – 3 A'S OF INTEGRITY, 3 C'S OF EMPATHY, and 3 T'S OF INTERACTION – all of which, when blended together, form a solid base upon which our strong, steady lives are built.

## *The 3 A's Of Integrity: Our Whole, Complete State*

Our integrity – a process of ACKNOWLEDGING, ACCEPTING, AND ACTING – propels us passionately through our lives.

# 1. We Acknowledge Ourselves

## We Acknowledge That We Are All Geniuses

With our unique wisdom, intellect, curiosity, creative power, and natural ability, we are all born to imagine and wonder, as we muster up immense strength to pursue our dreams, one by one, until they become a reality.

In our lifetimes, points of reference fluctuate when it comes to comparing or assessing everything within us and around us, so there is no solid measurement that says that only some of us possess incredible standards of excellence. Deep down inside we know that every one of us is a genius in our own distinct way.

*Edna efficiently and effectively runs a home with five children, an aging father, and seven tortoises. With arms open wide to others, Edna's genius, amongst many other qualities, is time management, as she sticks her neck out and safeguards the survival of her family; creatures and all.*

We know that the act of simply 'growing through our life' requires genius abilities, and we acknowledge that we are all geniuses as we let loose and follow through on our ideas; from finding a good way of rolling up our toothpaste tube, to packing our luggage in a manner which keeps it under the weight limit, to organizing a program which enables special-needs children to attend a live concert, to engineering a heart-lung bypass machine, to designing an observation satellite for monitoring weather and climate.

We are all geniuses because we find the 'how'
as the achiever and winner in us takes a bow.

## We Acknowledge That We Don't All Have the Same Knowledge

Every day we take in tens of thousands of thoughts and store them in our brain which contains millions of gigabytes of memory. Then, we store the bits of information we want, or need to remember, in our more accessible mental files.

We understand that others know more than we do about music, transportation, anatomy, politics, and many other subjects, which does not mean they are smarter than we are; it just means that they are more familiar with the specific knowledge which they use regularly, or which they find interesting.

We are all packed to the brim of our brains with a huge variety of knowledge, which – because of who we are – we are able to share with every other superstar.

## 2. We Accept Ourselves

*Anderson walks onto the stage to give a presentation, when suddenly, as he glances down, he notices that there is a large rip in the front of his pants, below the knee. He nods three times (giving himself time to think about a response to this embarrassing situation), and then he steps up to the podium, points to the rip, and says, "Good evening every-one. I love things that have a flaw in them – a scratched cabinet, a dented car – I can relate to such things."*

*The audience laughs and settles in, knowing that Anderson has removed any doubt they may encounter about his honesty and candidness.*

## We Judge Ourselves as a Means of Self-Acceptance

Judging ourselves to form a caring and impartial opinion about who we are at any given time, helps us to take away denial and defenses about the imperfections we continually encounter, both inwardly and outwardly.

We acknowledge that, like our ancestors, we are all bright diamonds, reflecting different colours; not flawless, but perfect and sparkling, as the innovative achiever in us gives birth to an idea and sets out to do it, even if it's against the odds.

With a nod of our head, and the beat of our heart, we accept ourselves.

## 3. We Act With Joy

We acknowledge and accept who we are as we put into action: 1) our quest for water, food, sleep, and shelter, and 2) our desire to live a full and happy life, as the elated joy-seeker in us emboldens us into action.

Day after day, we take full responsibility for our actions, driven by our unique abilities and our moral sense of what's right and what's wrong, as we marvel, connect, produce, learn, and grow; knowing that our very existence has a significant, positive effect on the planet.

Integrity is our sail which catches gusts of unfolding life as we acknowledge, accept, and steer our course over endless, glistening turquoise oceans, taking away fear from others as we light a flare, toss them a life jacket, extend a hand, or carry them to shore.

We are all aligned with the stars, our beacons of hope, on our passionate journey through this wonderful, adventurous life.

## The 3 C's of Empathy: Our Mirroring and Sensitive State

Our empathy – a process of CONSIDERING, CONTEMPLATING, AND CARING – moves us meaningfully through our lives.

## 1. We Consider the Pain of Others

*Troy is a life coach, who, after working forty hours a week, one-on-one with clients, decides to work twenty hours a week with clients and the other twenty at a penitentiary, helping prisoners to recognise the debris on their paths, and to find ways to remove it. When Troy sits beside a prisoner, he always begins by saying, "Although your view of the world right now in this facility is obscured by bars, my view of who you truly are is unobscured, bright, and clear."*

Mirror neurons located in the frontal lobe of our brain help us to recognise the pain of others, which reflects within ourselves, triggering an awareness of concern, and a strong desire to help.

Our empathy is not selective. We don't feel for the cute puppy but not the flea-ridden racoon, we don't feel for the poor student in our child's school but not the child in a faraway village across the globe, we don't feel for the bird but not the bat.

## 2. We Contemplate

Our mirror neurons trigger memories of how we may have felt at various points in our lives, and all of these triggers give us a small glimpse into the pain we may currently be observing in others.

- We remember a time when we felt extremely hungry: the feeling of gnawing pangs, dizziness, and weakness.
- We remember a time when we felt highly anxious: the feeling of general panic, fatigue, and restlessness.

- We remember a time when we felt deeply sad: the feeling of emotional exhaustion, nausea, and hopelessness.
- We remember a time when we felt ultimately rejected: the feeling of mental confusion, despair, and embarrassment.

These are only a few examples of the numerous types of negative emotions that some of us experience every single day of our lives; morning, noon, and night.

Being within our feelings is a place where we can relate to the emotions of others, and where we can contemplate what their suffering must feel like. We have all had, and continue to have, small glimpses into the suffering of others. There are no obstructive barriers when it comes to our empathy.

## 3. We Care

As soon as our emotions are aroused through our mirror neurons, when we witness the pain of others, we feel an overwhelming urge to help, to enable, to relieve, to emotionally support, and to save. And we do.

*Clive has dementia. His wife, Sally, tends to his every need. In the summer, his niece, Ingrid, does all his gardening, creating a beautiful, peaceful haven for him to relax in. In the winter, his fourteen-year-old neighbour, Carter, shovels the snow on his driveway after every snowfall, and shares a hot chocolate with him afterwards. His friend from church, Bob, visits one day a week to play guitar and sing with him.*

*His friend from the Seniors Centre, Armaan, takes him to play snooker one day a week. His children and grandchildren visit often to share stories of love and laughter.*

*Clive is wrapped up in the beautiful aura of empathy, which increases all the joyful moments in his life, day by day.*

Our empathy is as pure as the meaning of the word itself: being within our feelings. It is the outward expression of our untainted, all-encompassing love, which drives us to consider, and feel the impact of obstacles that appear on others' paths, which then motivates us to lean across and gracefully remove as many as we can from them.

We are all candles, burning away
surrendering ourselves to show others the way.

## *The 3 T's of Interaction: Our Attentive and Cooperative State*

Our interaction – a process of TURNING UP, TUNING IN, and TRANSCENDING – carries us caressingly through our lives.

## *1. We Turn Up*

Our altruistic radar, located in our hard-wiring, is constantly on alert, detecting and tracking all those stuck on their journey and needing help; for their safety, their happiness, and their well-being. Our built-in tracking systems have a powerful, positive effect on the world as a whole, making it a better place for everyone to dwell.

*An open-air rock concert is interrupted by the sudden approach of a monstrous, dark storm cloud and bright flashes of lightning. The people who are sitting on the grass banks all react simultaneously— they quickly gather up their belongings, while at the same time their heads swivel this way and that to see who needs help gathering up their belongings, and also who needs help with children or seniors. Everyone needs to get to the area near the stage, which is sheltered under a concrete roof, as quickly as possible. Within a few minutes the entire audience is huddled together, safe.*

*The violent storm passes rapidly and everyone returns to their spots on the banks while the band strikes up again, singing an appropriate song, ". . . awakening our universal love; below, within, and high, high above . . ."*

The friend in us is on stand-by around the clock . . . scanning . . . scanning . . . ready to leap into action in the pursuit of keeping everyone moving with confidence, with joy, and in optimal safety and health; through pleasure and pain, through sunshine and rain.

## 2. We Tune In

Before helping others, we pay attention to their needs, and if necessary we listen carefully to them, tuning in to all their words and expressions. We do this by:

- Creating a sacred circle around us, where we reassure them that whatever they say is held in the deepest confidence
- Listening attentively; with quiet, calm patience
- Not fast-forwarding the stories they tell us, or jumping to conclusions about what happens next
- Acknowledging that we are hearing everything they say by remaining focused, by encouraging them with small unobtrusive gestures, and by recognizing their truths according to how they experience them

We tune into others by adjusting our frequencies until they can directly transmit to us, and we can hear them, and only them, within our safe, shielded circle.

## 3. We Transcend

When we interact with others, we move beyond our own personal thoughts and emotions which then become intermingled with the thoughts and emotions of others. This brings together everyone's natural tools which help keep us all safe and content, as we savour life's journey.

*Rory senses that Don is not feeling good, so when their platoon goes out on patrol, he makes sure he is behind Don, ready to help him, if necessary. Out in the bush Don starts teetering, and right away Rory steps forward to support him, as they continue along a dangerous path.*

44

*After a while, Don is the only one who suddenly spots the slight impression of a landmine in the sand, and he immediately alerts the platoon!*

*This sequence of events, namely that, through assistance, Don is able to keep going during the patrol, results in several lives being saved.*

Not only are we always on guard to protect ourselves from danger; we are also on guard to help others when obstacles lie waiting on their paths, which ultimately safeguards us all. We go over and beyond what is deemed normal, with all our interactions, because this is how we breathe.

Our integrity propels us passionately through our lives. Our empathy moves us meaningfully through our lives. Our interactions carry us caressingly through our lives. And this forms the solid foundation of who we are, and the majestic life we build for all humankind.

# RESPECT STARTS AT HOME

We are all here, together, at this moment in time, graced with the knowledge that our very existence is a by-product of human relations, woven together through romance, rapture, and responsibility.

## *Our Romance*

*"Will you be my partner in forming a magnificent union that is creative, productive, and awe-inspiring; a union that will stand the test of time?"* It sounds like a tall order, but in essence, this is what we strive for in our intimate relationships.

Just as we know and respect who we truly are, we do the same for our romantic partners by honouring their lineage, inviting their communication, enjoying their playfulness, encouraging their creativity, cherishing their love, embracing their open arms, joining in their explorations, supporting their artistry, admiring their collections, celebrating their victories, championing their achievements, participating in their joy-seeking, hoping and dreaming together, and welcoming all the doors which they open for us.

And throughout all these adoring, affectionate days, we offer each other time and space, to reflect, to learn, to grow, and to express in our own unique ways.

# Our Romantic Stories Are a Beautiful Dance

## We Spot Each Other

*The music begins. Our inner ear translates the sweet vibrations into signals that trigger feelings of intense pleasure.*

Our eyes meet. A spark of euphoric chemicals is ignited within us, as a deep, magnetic attraction composes a feeling of two worlds melding into one.

## We Make Our Way to the Dance Floor

*The music washes over us. We head to the dance floor, with hands clasped, stopping briefly to greet, and meet people, as well as to move aside anything obstructing our way.*

We commit our love to each other. Our love deepens as we date, get to know each other, support each other, clear the path for each other, and prioritize our relationship to reach a harmonious union.

## We Dance

*We become the music. We move in unison, working together with each other's frames, strengths, and rhythms, as we step, sway, and swirl, every now and then our eyes wandering off in all directions, but always returning to gaze deeply into each other's hearts.*

We merge our lives together through cohabitation or marriage as we embrace the new expanse of our unified lives; settling in, deep within, as we:

- travel to vast glaciers together; enjoying panoramic views and introspection
- huddle around crackling fires together; thawing out icy beliefs and judgments
- climb majestic mountains together; achieving new heights of enlightenment
- star-gaze together; creating, and considering future possibilities

Music unites us
two dancers melded into one
forming a union that *will* stand the test of time
as we step *in* time with one another
under a glorious, golden sun.

## We are Team Players in Our Relationships

*Two married accountants, Gail and Hudson, always manage their combined home finances together, and then when Hudson becomes overwhelmed at work with his new promotion to Chief Financial Officer, Gail offers to manage the home finances alone and give Hudson a monthly printout of where they stand.*

*Hudson responds, "My sweet Gail, I gratefully take you up on your offer. However, when it comes to tax time,*

*I offer to 'fire up the file' because, as you know, everything in our accounting worlds must be balanced."*

When we are in an intimate relationship, we know that we can reach in easily to 'take from each other,' and, being a good team, to leave each other with a smooth road to travel on, where we can balance our lives as we follow every dream.

## We Embrace All Ages in Our Relationships

*When Errol proposes to Sarah, who is twenty-one years younger than him, Sarah's reasoning to her family and friends is, "If Errol can give me at least ten years of happiness, and vice-versa, then why would I not take it?"*
*Errol and Sarah get married, have two wonderful sons, and live happily together for over thirty years.*

In our life stories, we experience various chapters of our lives at various times. However, the theme of all our stories, which reflects who we truly are, is 'timeless.' An older partner is still an infant, a teenager, and a young adult, and we cherish this factual narrative as we page through their story, tenderly embracing every word, paragraph, and chapter.

The collector in us gathers and treasures friends and partners of all ages, so that we can experience all the many amazing chapters in each other's lives:

- how we have all hit roadblocks
- how we have all felt euphoric and joyful
- how we have all united people
- how we have all had to pick up the pieces of our broken hearts
- how we all love the world we live in

Regardless of all the chapter endings in our lives – including our youth – our story goes on, and on, because our true core is a strong book binding that never decays or ages. There is no end to who we truly are. We are ageless, vibrant beings.

# FAMILY: A STEADY BEDROCK OF TOGETHERNESS AND RESPECT

Our togetherness begins with our strong will
to build homes, to nurture families,
and to live life to the full.

## *Our Names*

From the day we were born we have constantly heard our name: *"Hello little Meggy," "Paddy Pat, look here,"* so our name has a large circuit in our brain that becomes instantly activated upon hearing it; linking us to our identity, and especially to our uniqueness.

We respect others by saying their names frequently to show them that they are seen, acknowledged, considered, and valued, for who they are in this wonderful, homey world which we live in. And although the prefix to all our names is silent, it is there, loud and clear: VIP.

## *Relatives: We Have More than One Home*

*Svetlana, a children's book writer and illustrator, is not born in her parents' homeland, but she always expresses a strong connection to it in her words and drawings. When political instability sweeps across the homeland, causing a huge shortage of food and medicine, Svetlana does some research, connects with her distant family there, and sends them three thousand dollars from her savings, to help them through their challenging times.*

*One week later, Svetlana receives a response from a publisher about a manuscript and drawings she submitted, and, as she reads the details of the response, an enormous sense of connection stirs within her. The publisher is offering her a three thousand dollar advance for her book.*

*Although Svetlana has never physically met her distant relatives, she takes away some of their strife, so that all of her relatives, on both continents, are left with a deep knowing that they all have a home with one another.*

Our relatives, connected by a loving line of descent – whether they are known to us or not – are an expansion of ourselves, as they refresh, restore, revitalize, and reconnect us on our journey through life.

- Our relatives who dwell in cities refresh us with a sense of fascination, convenience, and endless possibilities
- Our relatives who dwell on farms restore us with a sense of value, clarity, and self-reliance
- Our relatives who dwell in cabins revitalize us with a sense of awakening, calmness, and grounding
- Our relatives who dwell in colonies reconnect us with a sense of sharing, security, and belonging

Like ocean currents, our compassion flows easily and freely through our bloodline, which continues to flush out blockages as it transports love all over the globe.

## *We Give Birth with a Long, Deep Sigh*

Our relationships undergo a huge reconstruction when there are births in our families, which require us to reinforce our lives with new, powerful layers of altruism.

As it is with all animals, we are born altruistic, giving of ourselves so that others have their natural needs met; sharing food like apes do, offering comfort to newborns like earwigs do, protecting babies like birds do.

When there are births in our families, we see our whole future in our newborn's eyes, as the ancestor in us celebrates the fruits of their labour, and the baby in us smiles gleefully as they reach, reach, reach out their arms.

## *We Raise Our Families on the Podium of Respect*

Our children are born with powerful senses, the most important being the sense of belonging, and we all understand that it is our role to nurture this crucial, life-preserving sense as we guide our children on how to live and thrive happily, in *their* particular time, in *their* particular place on Earth. One of the ways we do this is by keeping them safe and supporting them through their growth and development, while at the same time clearing the way for them to form their own harmless and fair views, whenever they are faced with incoming impressions.

Families share multiple things: books, shampoo, cousins, salt, laughter, tears, strengths and vulnerabilities, values and beliefs. And when it comes to parenting, we all have different parenting styles focused on what we feel we need to teach our children: independence, love of nature, street-smarts, strength, patriotism, among others.

Like great, devoted gardeners, some of us raise our families to resemble a manicured garden: traditional, organized, and well-maintained, with stunning shrubs and handsome fences, and some of us raise our families to resemble a wild garden: left mostly to nature with a mishmash of wildflowers, grass and weeds, and with some secretive nooks and space for wildlife to creep in. This variety of gardens makes for a beautiful, variegated, colourful, well-functioning world.

*Carl says of his parents: "My father makes my world turn around; my mother helps me to stay on it."*

We all need time and space to co-operatively, and also independently, live our lives to the fullest. With that in mind, we respect our family members' time and space as we continually share with each other, and support each other, so that we can all reach positive, productive middle-ground settlements in our homes.

We are born with our integrity, our empathy, and our ingrained ability to interact, and within our family life – be it with genetically-related people, or otherwise – we step up to the podium of respectfulness, around the clock, as we dig, and plant, and smile proudly.

## Loving Our Siblings

Our long, long relationships with our brothers and sisters are priceless because, right from birth, we hold up mirrors to each other, so that we can see our own behaviours which guide us on how to share and care, how to comprehend verbal and non-verbal communication, and how to select the safest and sunniest roads to travel on.

The reflections we see in these mirrors are a valuable tool which we add to our tool bag because, as we venture along, we can see our floods of feelings, our states of mind, and our sequences of actions. Then, based on these reflections, we can choose to either flail, lurch, and heave, or we can paddle harder, or in some cases we can simply relax and float upon the wild and wonderful waves of life.

Siblings also hold up rearview mirrors to each other, reflecting treasured memories of togetherness and love. And also, for those of us who believe in seeing our future in mirrors, our siblings play a significant role in helping us to get glimpses of what lies on our road ahead.

Brothers and sisters – full, half, step, or adopted –
are dynamic characters in our story
as they care, as they share
and as they remain by our side
always, and everywhere.
. . . reflecting . . . reflecting . . .

## *Loving Our Adopted Children*

As it is with many animals – like faithful albatrosses, protective tigers, and warm-hearted sea lions – we humans offer a sincere sense of belonging to a fostered or adopted child, which ensures their safety and security, while reinforcing their awareness of the power of connectivity.

During the adoption process, the confident dreamer in us negotiates multiple wise, intuitive agreements, which result in us experiencing overwhelming joy and fulfilment for being offered the opportunity to carry out this great-hearted deed, as we settle in to do some major reconstruction.

This is also a time when we empathize with ourselves and with others equally, feeling the loss suffered all around – perhaps the loss of a family lineage, or the loss of future dreams of raising one's own children, and so on – however, the nurturing parent within all of us guides us gracefully through the adoption process as we all remain focused on the young, playful child, who lights up their own life, and who inspires others to do the same.

When we go through the process of adopting a child, we take much away from ourselves – loneliness, yearning, unfulfillment – as we make room for 1) the glorious birth of the 'unification with a needing child' and 2) the primal and arousing emotions that flood our being as we hold our child for the first time.

We also take much away from our adopted child – insecurity, misplacement, uncertainty – as we remind them of the wonderful array of natural tools that they possess, in order to live and blossom in this beautiful world where we all belong. Them. Us. And Everyone.

## *Loving Our Adoptive Parents*

When we are adopted, we understand that the adoption process unfolds with a huge investment of faith and strength from our birth parents, as well as from our adoptive parents:

- Our birth parents have enough faith to accept that they are unable to care for us, and they have enough strength to offer us to someone who can
- Our adoptive parents have enough faith to accept that they will be able to care for us, and they have enough strength to raise us as their own

All four parents toss their own uncertainties, doubts, and fears aside, leaving room for parental altruism to step in; namely, the unconditional offering of mercy, tenderness, and love for a child in need, and ultimately this takes away any insecurities which an adopted child may have to face as they mature.

The act of adopting children confirms that the nurturing parent in all of us is alive and well, and it will never rest until every child on Earth is given the chance to experience who they truly are. Adoption is as natural as nature itself.

## *Love in Our Family Homes*

Our family homes are filled with a kaleidoscope of lovely auras, which are electromagnetic fields that radiate from within the many energy centers of our bodies: fiery fearless reds, adventurous oranges, calm yellows, nurturing greens, intuitive blues, curious indigos, and crisp, creative violets.

In our homes, built on strong foundations, we guide each other in positive directions, while removing challenging obstacles that appear on our paths, so that we can all remain upright and strong, allowing our auras to radiate bright and free around us.

As we gaze upward, we see all the colourful auras in our family homes reflected above our rooftops in the form of glowing rainbows; beautiful arcs which represent the unity of support and strength of all who dwell within.

## We Offer Each Other 'Symbolic' Rooms for Creativity and Growth

We are continually inspecting our family homes, and stepping aside as we invite each other to occupy various 'symbolic' rooms where, at various points in our lives, we can find clarity and self-discover, where we can harness our strength and self-empower, and where we can define our goals and plan our next moves, one after another.

We may offer a hallway to someone who is entering a new phase in their lives, or a living room to someone who is in the process of reconnecting with others. We may offer a basement to someone for transformation, or a kitchen for nurturing. Or we may offer a bedroom for recharging, or a bathroom for purifying, or an attic for spiritual growth.

Our family homes are where we plant, nourish, and reap an abundant harvest of passion and prosperity, set on a steady bedrock of togetherness and respect, in a well-maintained house of love.

## We Always Find Ways to Compliment a Person's Home

*On a social networking website, a collage of sunny beaches is posted, followed by at least fifty comments of a similar tone:*

~   *"My memories of that place are priceless."*

~ *"I used to love those beaches, but because we immigrated, sadly those days are now over."*
~ *"I'm glad the generations of today are experiencing the great times we once enjoyed there."*

We know, at the bottom of our hearts, that like everything, areas of our Earth do change, affected by tides and weather, erosion and deposits, disrepair, development, and many more, and this is when we carefully consider that 'everywhere is home to someone' as we show our respect and affection towards their place of safety, love, unity, treasured memories, and overhead rainbows.

When we embrace a person's home, we embrace *them*.

# RESPECT KEEPS OUR FOUNDATION STRONG THROUGH ALL OF LIFE'S CHALLENGES

## *Loving Through Relationship Breakups*

In life we are either sailing away from one storm, or heading into another, as we glance back, and gaze forward. Some storms shake us about; others devastate. And in between these storms, thank the stars, we can sometimes experience a moment of smooth sailing.

In the early days of wooden ships, beautiful church pews were made from the wood of washed-up wrecks. Divorces can be shipwrecks, but the confident dreamer in us quickly gathers up all the debris from the wrecks and uses it to rebuild our lives, to the point of being able to sit comfortably, stand steadily, sing happily, and kneel in gratitude.

After we bid farewell to a relationship, we take our helm, hoist our sails, and then we embark into new, uncharted waters that invite us into a world of power, possibility, and hope.

*After signing her divorce papers, Kimberly decides to write her divorce vows, which she shares with Mark.*

*"I, Kimberly West, take you, Mark Fraser, to be my ex-husband, to live apart as an unwed couple, in separate homes, from this day forward. I promise to preserve good memories and nurture our joint family; for better, for worse, for richer, for poorer, in sickness and in health, until death do us part.*

*I promise to focus fully on my own new beginnings and relationships throughout my present and future life, as I remain faithful to my divorce vows, by creating a healthy heart, mind, and soul, as long as we both shall live."*

As we say goodbye to others who have travelled by our side for some time, we skip off the dance floor and leave them with their pride.

> We are all unique, on our own journey
> as we sail onward and free
> over endless, glistening oceans
> towards our new, true destiny.

## We are Designed to Accept Love, No Matter What

Sometimes on life's journey, because of obstacles on our road, we may come upon a sign which reads, 'LOVE IS NOT FORTHCOMING TO YOU RIGHT NOW.' As we explore our thoughts, we understand the reasons why this sign may appear:

~ *"Everyone else is more important than I am."*
This is when our self-esteem has dipped slightly, and we feel that our own needs are secondary to the needs of others.

This is also when we open our hearts, and, often with the help of others, we wipe our windshield to give ourselves a brighter, broader view of who we truly are; fully deserving of all the love that swirls around our planet.

~ *"I can't handle another loss."*
This is when we feel traumatized after losing someone we love through various reasons, such as a break-up, an abandonment, a death, and so forth.

This is also when we come out of our dark rooms and, often with the help of others, we allow bright light to permeate through us, illuminating who we truly are; fully deserving of all the love that radiates around the globe.

There are many reasons why we may feel that we don't deserve love at certain points in our lives, and this may prompt us to build a solid fortress around ourselves to keep us strong, proud, and protected, so that we don't have to face what the Raiders of Pain will bring to us if we allow love to enter.

This is when we glance at the 'LOVE IS NOT FORTH-COMING TO YOU RIGHT NOW' sign and we rejuvenate our trust; trust that even if we feel that love will fail us again, we have the strength to rebound and get back on our journey.

We help others through the gridlocks of insecurity and distress, with our empathy, as we consider their pain, as we contemplate on how they may feel, and as we care for them, while we walk beside them; lighting their way to the remembrance and adulation of who they truly are, and how deserving they are of love.

We are all composed of layer upon layer of exceptional qualities, which gives us the ability to love, and to accept love, for the entire duration of our journey through life.

## *We Embrace All Personalities*

Our personalities are our monitors; large expressive and descriptive screens that are visible to everyone around us, showing scenes of drama, comedy, mystery, adventure, and much more. These screens reveal our egos – our inner selves – displaying our individual needs, reaffirming our values, and expressing how we feel about our day-to-day, and overall life. Our personalities are predictable, structured, and always reliable.

*When the DuPlooy family decide to do a fire drill in their home, Dirk, the father, lays out a moment-to-moment plan of what to do when an alarm goes off, and, as he hugs everyone, he reassures them that he will continue to check all safety in the home, and that no harm will ever come to them.*

*Lara, the mother, does several hours of research, and buys a new, up-to-date supply of smoke and carbon monoxide detectors as she reassures everyone that they've got this.*

*Evi, the daughter, sets up a white notice board with lots of colourful stickers, draws a map of the house, and hands everyone a dry erase marker so they can outline their tasks.*

*Johannes, the son, leads everyone around the house and points out where the extinguishers are located as he demonstrates how to operate them, and where all the smoke detectors are and how to check that they are working, and how to change the batteries, and so on.*

*After the family finishes the very successful fire drill, they all pat Frikkie, the dog, on the head and say, "Ya Frikkie, you know you're in this plan with us because, bro, you are one of the best fire alarms around."*

Our various personalities keep our world safe, happy, and thriving, as we collectively tackle all of life's challenges with a large variety of ideas brought to the table.

We all possess most of the qualities of every personality

type, however some of us put extreme focus into certain areas, which collectively contributes to the high-functioning world we live in.

- There are those who focus on nurturing – diligent, dependable, and perceptive of others – always excelling at comfort and care. We love these people by taking away any stress they might have so that they can focus on serving those in need.

- There are those who focus on organization – reliable, responsible, and trusting of others – always following a set plan. We love these people by taking away any constraints they might have so that they can focus on getting everything to work in sync.

- There are those who are artistically inspired – sensitive, original, and deep in thought – always enhancing the beauty surrounding them. We love these people by taking away any self-doubt they might have so that they can focus on their creativity as they visually teach, and please everyone.

- There are those who are hands-on motivated – analytical, realistic, and straight-forward – always excelling to find solutions to problems. We love these people by taking away any distractions they might have so that they can focus on making everything run smoothly in the world.

We know who we all truly are, and we embrace one another with open arms, and then, when it comes to our vast array of personalities, we tilt our heads to one side, and with a little nod and a smile, we extend our arms even further to embrace the wonderful mosaic of colourful characters which make our world far more interesting, multidimensional, and enchanting, than it would be if it was inhabited by billions of cookie-cutter beings.

## We Choose Assistance Over Negative Judgement

*Emma Jane invites four of her friends to visit her ninety-three-year-old grandmother, Ida, in a nursing home. Before the visit, Emma Jane tells her friends that Ida may say a few things that are not politically correct, and she reassures them that she will take care of it.*

*The visit is filled with hilarious story-telling and merry laughter, even though Ida blurts out 'politically incorrect' words and phrases here and there. Emma Jane and her friends do not want to interrupt Ida's story-telling, so they simply take a deep breath and ignore all the improprieties.*

*After the visit, once her friends leave, Emma Jane stays behind and writes down all the 'politically incorrect' words and phrases used, and together she and Ida discuss how, and why they are currently less spoken.*

*Ida is fascinated, and she begins to understand how certain words can be seen as marginalizing, and discriminating, and as Emma Jane gets up to leave she says, "Thank you for keeping me up to date with our positively-changing world, Emmy darling, and also, on a personal note, thank you for not embarrassing me in front of your friends."*

*Emma Jane knows that Ida's time is short and very precious, therefore she never marginalizes her for not keeping up with the times, and she never discriminates against her generation. Instead, whenever Emma Jane spends time with her grandmother, she takes away any obstacles that may damage her dignity, as well as any obstacles that may prevent her from telling her vivid and noteworthy tales, which give Ida a powerful sense of purpose and meaning, and which give Emma Jane a powerful sense of courage and honour.*

When we see incorrectness, we rub our eyes
around and around
until a clear, authentic image
is ultimately found.

## Dignity, Like Gently Rolling Ripples, Spreads Infectiously Through Our Communities

*Alice is browsing around the fresh produce in her local supermarket when suddenly she slips on something wet and tumbles to the ground! She hears gasps all around and the next moment, as a burning pain grips her leg, four customers appear and stare down at her, bombarding her with questions:*

*"Are you hurt?"*
*"Are you okay?"*
*"Did you trip?"*
*"Are you alright?"*

*This attracts even more well-meaning customers to amass, and stare, and ask questions. A staff member appears, phones for medical help, and gives details of the problem and the location.*

*A young man edges his way through the crowd, slithers down to sit beside Alice, and with his hand placed gently on Alice's forearm he says, "Hi, so this is what Mateo's Market looks like from down here. I'm Jamar. What's your name?" Moments pass . . . "I am going to sit right here with you, dear Alice, under the fresh and friendly fiddleheads, until help arrives."*

*Help soon does arrive, and as Alice is being carried out of Mateo's Market on a stretcher, she turns her head to smile at Jamar, the one who, although not qualified to offer medical assistance, shows true love by taking away her awkwardness and embarrassment as he joins her on the soggy, slippery floor.*

Like gently rolling ripples, stirred up by our integrity and empathy, we are continually moving outward, outward, ready to remove uneasiness and embarrassment from one another, when obstacles suddenly cause us to slip, and tumble.

## *The Little Things We Do for Large Results*

When we are children, we love 'reward' play, when small amounts of impact are required to create huge results; like skateboarding, swinging, any form of wheels, or jumping on a mattress.

As we interact with others, small actions or comments show others that they are not alone when it comes to any missteps on their journey:

- *"I know, I keep forgetting where I parked my car, too."*
- *"We all make those kinds of mistakes, like the time when I got on the bus and I looked down and, would you believe it, I was wearing one black boot and one brown boot!"*

One of the most impactful ways that we help to clear each other's life paths, is when we say simple 'relating' lines that remove self-doubt, and dramatically boost dignity, which is one of the key elements in the foundation of all our relationships.

An ordinary coin tossed into a pond
creates extraordinary effects
as it ripples on and on.

# Our Points of View, Suggestions, and Advice, are Simply Information Signs

We are all teachers on Earth – every one of us, young and old – as we offer points of view, suggestions, and advice to one another, based on our own past experiences, present observations, and future predictions.

We know that it is impossible to make others think and act like we do, because we are all unique, however, based on our own experiences and/or knowledge about certain things, we love each other by politely and respectfully holding up information signs on each other's roads which read:

- MY POINT OF VIEW: *This is how I see the challenge; perhaps you can see it this way too.*
- MY SUGGESTION: *This is what I believe can work; perhaps you can believe it too.*
- MY ADVICE: *This is what has helped others in this case; perhaps it can help you too.*

From *"How about trying their new Christmas cake; it is merrilicious,"* to *"Why don't you ask her to meet, where you can discuss a positive road, moving forward,"* to *"If you follow the health statistics on this ailment, you will be cured within a few months,"* . . . our information signs, when utilized, can clear the path for others, as they pull out old weeds (old negative, non-productive brain neurons) and free up brain space where they can cultivate a lovely, lush garden (new positive, fruitful brain neurons); if not with actions, then at least with new skills, new knowledge, and new understanding.

We gracefully and gratefully accept points of view, suggestions, and advice from each other because we know that it is an expression of care and love, and also because the more tools we acquire for living, the more endowed we become.

As we journey along our road, whenever necessary, we hold up information signs to others, which is simply a way of sharing all the experience and knowledge circulating throughout our world. This is what we know *does* work.

## We Allow Others to Choose to Not Choose

*Rita is in a meeting with her co-workers when a workplace question arises. Everyone in the meeting speaks about the problem, solutions, or what they would like to see happen, etc. and then when it comes to Rita's turn, she politely says, "I have no comment at this point," to which her colleagues politely reply, "That is absolutely fine, Rita. If ever, or whenever you are ready, we are here to try to answer any questions that you may have."*

We are gentle, we are wise. Every day, as thousands of questions lap our raft – smacking it, splashing it, waiting for answers – our compass guides us to choose wisely. We know that we do not have to comment on every conversation, or answer every question put to us. We know that we have the choice to say *"Yes"* or *"No"* and in many cases, because we are not informed enough or we need more time to process it, to say, *"I have no opinion about it."*

When others do not have the answers, we respect them by taking away expectations, knowing that we all have the choice to not choose, as we float along, gracefully relaxing with the rolling tide.

## We Gain a Broader View of Life as We Rise Up in Our Hot Air Balloons

There are times when we crawl around Earth's surface like little ants, only able to see the obstacles that stand directly in front of us. This is when we take a huge breath and fire up our hot air balloons as we rise higher . . . higher . . . to a position where we are able to get a more panoramic view of the land; to the north, east, south, and west of our stumbling blocks.

This wider perception enables us to seek alternative routes to new perspectives and possibilities, as we witness the truth about every vibrant being who inhabits our planet; how heroic, resilient, and kind-hearted we all are, and how we are here for one another, near and afar.

## We Offer Simple Solutions to Those Who Cannot Fire Up Their Hot Air Balloons

When someone cannot fill their balloon with hot air because they don't have the expertise, the experience, or the energy to do so, we step forward and gently take away their immobility by offering them easy-to-follow, simple solutions:

- *"There are great courses available to learn the language of your new country."*
- *"There are great support groups available for you during your grieving process."*
- *"There are great self-help groups available to help in your addiction recovery process."*

Then, after a time, as we see their wonderful, weightless balloons soaring up high in the bright blue sky, we wave to let them know that we will be there upon their return, when they are back on solid ground, embraced by their friendly colony, where they can once again focus on their journey ahead.

## We Are All Conductors of the Human Symphony

*When Hao goes out for a walk to an unexplored part of his town, he comes across a large stretch of community gardens. He stops to talk to a few of the gardeners who are perspiring profusely in the scorching heat. He asks why a lot of the gardens are dry and dusty and not cultivated, and when the gardeners tell him that the town promised to deliver topsoil and fertilizer several weeks before, which has still not arrived, Hao promises that he will try to help.*

*Hao is very well connected in the municipality, and after making several phone calls, he gets reassurance that the task of delivering the necessary requirements to the gardens will be done.*

*Three days later Hao is seen approaching the community gardens, carrying a basket of sliced, juicy watermelon, and bottles of chilled water, which he hands out to the gardeners who are extremely busy turning over fresh, rich topsoil and fertilizer, to the sound of a Koto musical instrument being played under a large maple tree.*

*Hao takes away his townsfolk's sweat of disconnect as he connects them to suppliers, so that their crops can be cultivated, harvested, and shared.*

We are all kind, loving friends, the great conductors of a living symphony, creating tempo and rhythm and grand finales, as we seek solutions to everyone's needs. We move, and harmonise the world around us, to produce the magnificent masterpiece called LIFE.

## *We Act in Fairness*

Our universe is divided up into hot and cold gases, energy, and matter. Our planet is divided up into land and water. All these divided components give us the functional and meticulous life as we know it. And this, in turn, programs each one of us to reach out and divide our love fairly between everyone and everything. And this, in turn, gives each of us purpose and meaning, which collectively translates into a glorious, stabilised existence.

We take turns at four-way stops and merging into traffic, we pack equal-sized gift boxes for the poor, we divide our energy and time equally between family members and friends, and much, much more. Our divided deeds are infinite. Our fairness is a quality which keeps everything balanced on our roads of life:

- We subtract our self-interest. Add our humanity. Divide our capabilities. And multiply our good deeds.
- We subtract our biases. Add our impartiality. Divide our awareness. And multiply our love.

We are all the square root of each other, our earth, and our universe. We are fair.

## Our Respect Is Handed out to Everyone in Equal Quantities

From the person who scrubs city sewers or sells their wares on a sidewalk, to the person who runs a water treatment plant or manages a retail store, to the president of a country or a foreign ambassador, to the leader of a religious order or the head of a global organization; we respect everyone equally, for their contribution and their strength, as we place an exquisite crown upon their head to symbolize our gratitude, our pride, and our highest respect.

One size crown fits ALL.

## Love and All Its Parts

All of us who inhabit this magnificent planet do not see each other as disposable commodities. *"My friend is driving me crazy with this phase he's going through; I think I'll just dump him." "I hardly talk to my mother anymore; she's out of control."* Instead of seeing others this way, we either:

1. Step forward to remove any obstacles in their path, or

2. Cherish and respect them as wonderful, living, breathing beings, or

3. There is no 3

Respect – the solid, immovable bedrock of all our relationships, built with three potent ingredients – speaks loudly, as we use all our tools to perceive, accept, empathize, help, and honour one another.

Our respect is divided equally for ourselves and for others, as we honour names and birthdays, homes and families, relatives, friends, acquaintances, townsfolk, countrymen, and intercontinental peers; preserving the dignity in all.

With our powerful foundations, magnificent houses are built, so that together, forever, we flourish.

# PART TWO

# THE WALLS

Memories and experiences make up the walls,
which aren't always straight or perfect.
Some are flimsy, some are temporary, and some are solid.
The walls are there to hold up our relationships
and define the various stages of our lives,
which are forever changing;
often working with us, sometimes working against us.

When Experience speaks, it says, *"I understand that life is ever-evolving and I accept where everyone is on their journey. I will always be there to apply my knowledge to help you to live your life to the fullest as you hang up beautiful photographs from the past, as you move through doorways to explore more areas, and as you open windows to let in light, and beauty, and fresh clean air, so that together, forever, we will advance."*

## *We Have All Been Given Our Own Private Beach of Time*

As we all walk along our beautiful beaches of time, our toes caress the cool, soft sand where small ocean waves nuzzle up to us, and then hiss away. Behind us the sky is dark and forgotten as we leave our past behind. Ahead, eastward, the sky shimmers shell pink, and slowly, in time, a glowing red ball pulsates on the horizon as we remain focused on our hopes and dreams.

We inhale the briny tang of the ocean as it rises and falls like a mighty chest, and as the sticky, salty air washes over us, we feel the adherent connection to everyone, and everything.

There are times in our lives when our beaches are long, and wide, and filled with sand; times when we are able to keep the shore well-dredged and free of debris, so that we can continue to explore and grow with every step we take.

There are also times in our lives when large waves wash in, shortening and narrowing our beaches, depleting our time, often leaving widely scattered debris on the shore.

This is when we bring out all our tools to remove the debris and begin the dredging process; sucking up soil from the ocean floor and depositing it onto our beach, to widen our shoreline and expand our time.

When our beaches are narrow and cluttered
others walk beside us to help remove debris and grime
as we leave many trails of footprints
on our beautiful, private beaches of time.

## *The Rhythm of Our Lives*

The Earth is powered by rhythms: four bright, bountiful seasons, ebbing and flowing tides, daytime, nighttime, and an orbiting moon, creating perfect harmony worldwide.

These predictable global rhythms give us an organized timeline to regulate and manage our day-to-day existence, as well as a soothing sense of security that safeguards us all.

All living things are propelled by rhythms: military marching, drummers drumming, bullfrogs croaking, horses trotting, workers chanting, athletes jogging. These rhythms steady us and connect us to each other, motivating us to survive, to thrive, and to celebrate being alive.

Our bodies function brilliantly through rhythmic processes: breathing, heartbeat, twenty-four-hour sequences of alertness and sleepiness, menstrual cycles, and many, many more, and, as babies, our sense of security is reaffirmed by the rhythm of relaxing, restful rocking, side to side to side to side . . .

*Carl does not sleep well; he is worried that his snoring will wake up Edna. Edna does not sleep well; she is worried that Carl's snoring will wake her up.*

*Neither Carl nor Edna wants to upset each other's sleeping rhythms, so every night, one of them gets up at any given hour and goes to sleep on the couch in the living-room, until one night Carl creeps downstairs and flops onto the couch right on top of Edna!*

*They both laugh out loud and decide that it is now time to make a 'royal' plan – get a sleep divorce – where separate bedrooms become the solution.*

*The loving friends in Carl and Edna take away the disruption of each other's Master clocks, which keep a twenty-four-hour rhythm within us, to help us to sleep soundly throughout the night.*

Timing is the first thing we consider when we interact with each other. Just like rainbows which show us that, with the correct timing, rhythm, balance, and positioning, breathtaking beauty can radiate from all things.

## *The Rhythmic Effect of Music Unites Us All*

Whether we are humming alone while sweeping, or we are singing out loud in the shower, we are united with others; either with the original singers of a song, or with the composers and musicians of a musical piece.

As we sing, we release happy little peace-giving messenger molecules in our bodies, which build our trust in ourselves, in each other, and in the whole world. This steady confidence unites us all in a surge of loving emotions that transport us to a faraway landscape; so sunny, so enchanting.

*It is a hot summer's day when Layla's friends gather to hold a Celebration of Life after her passing. Everyone is sitting on deck chairs scattered around Layla's back yard, and then, when someone starts singing Layla's favourite song about wind stirring up emotions, everyone jumps up, shuffles into a circle, grabs onto each other's hands, and together they sing the song out loud, with immense passion and love.*

*Suddenly a strong breeze starts blowing, swirling around and around the back yard, and tosses everyone's hats off their heads, whirling them around and around . . . And then, as fast as the breeze starts, it stops.*

*Layla's friends hurry off to search for their hats, and when they find them, they pick them up, hold them to their chests, and smile, as powerful emotions are stirred up within their hearts.*

Whether we are belting out rock songs, solemnly singing hymns, or chanting OM, music takes away our feelings of isolation, and, as all our rhythms begin to synchronise with each other, a resounding unification of our collective true selves is felt, and expressed, in celebration of our wonderful, windswept world.

In the beautiful dance of life
we all keep in time
as all our natural rhythms resonate
and align.

# WE ARE MINDFUL OF TIMING AS WE LOVE

## *We Consider the Various Ages of Those We Help*

We consider the various ages, as well as the various stages of others' lives, which helps us to understand how best to interact with them on multiple levels.

When we interact with INFANTS AND CHILDREN, we are nurturing and reassuring, taking away any discomfort or insecurities which they may be experiencing.

*When Devon spots a little boy roaming around the aquarium by himself, he goes over to him and says, "Hello young man, my name is Devon and I am going to help you find your mom, or dad. And then, you know what? Very, very soon they are going to wave at you and call out, 'Whoa, of course, there's our favourite sea horse!'"*

When we interact with ADOLESCENTS AND ADULTS, we are supportive and encouraging, taking away any anxiety and hopelessness which they may be experiencing.

*When Stan and Rhonda lose their business during a market crash, as they browse through items at the local food bank, a stranger who is there dropping off items, hands them both a business card with a note which reads: "If it's something you require, I would be honoured to interview you for a job with my affluent company."*

*Within seven days both Stan and Rhonda are once again employed, by R. Finch (aka the stranger), and within seven months they are both back at the food bank, dropping off items.*

When we interact with SENIORS, we are attentive and respectful, taking away any incompetence and loneliness which they may be experiencing.

*John sits alone in the corner of the recreation room in the long-term care home, while everyone else chats away merrily in groups; some at the card table, others lingering around the lunch table. Denis, a volunteer, goes over to John and asks him three questions:*

*"How many children do you have?"*

*"What's your favourite pastime?"*

*"What line of work were you in?"*

*After John answers the questions, Denis wheels him over to the group around the card table and says, "Excuse me everyone, did you know that John here has eight children, he loves making garden gnomes, and he was involved in the building of Naman Towers on Copper Street West back in the early sixties?"*

*After a while, Denis sits watching as John plays cards, surrounded by loving gestures and sincere, exuberant laughter, as everyone in the group cuddles closer to him, wanting to know more and more about this wonderful, fascinating man.*

We embrace the various ages of everyone around us, because although we may not have experienced a certain age ourselves, as loving friends, we naturally open our arms to understanding and acceptance, and our hearts to loyalty and love.

## *We Are Aware of the Times When a Metamorphosis Is in Progress*

Like waves in the ocean, circumstances continuously wash onto our shore, sometimes unfurling gracefully, sometimes crashing with a thunderous roar.

For many of us, a metamorphosis, or radical personal transformation, can occur more than once in our lifetime, regardless of our age. This is when our familiar life begins to fall away, and a new, unexplored life begins to emerge.

At any given time, we could be at the stage of a lowly caterpillar, or we could be at the stage where we are withdrawn into a light, shiny chrysalis, or we could be at the point in our lives where we have transformed into a beautiful, soaring butterfly, which is a symbol of freedom and rebirth.

1. THE CATERPILLAR: This is the learning and developmental stage of our existence, when day by day we crawl and wiggle along, eating up life in large quantities and storing energy; focused only on what is directly in front of us as we relocate and decorate our walls.

2. THE CHRYSALIS: This is when something happens which has a huge impact on us: a loss, a bankruptcy, a deceit, or perhaps we simply grow restless.

We surrender. We retract. We ground ourselves and begin to weave a sturdy chrysalis around and around us; a protective shield like our great planet possesses, to protect it from incoming meteoroids that break up in the atmosphere before they strike the surface.

Our transformation begins, which may include dissolving our limiting beliefs, educating ourselves, or tapping into our infinite potential as we ponder new possibilities.

However we feel during the chrysalis stage, as we hang suspended in time . . . unwavering . . . floating . . . releasing . . . we give ourselves up fully, with a deep knowing that a resurrection of our true, liberated self, will eventually emerge.

This dismantling process may be a terrifying, or vulnerable time for us, or it may be a gentle and steadfast passage into new, lush pastures.

3. THE LIBERATION: We know when we are ready to emerge from our isolation, and our breath deepens . . . in . . . out . . . in . . . out . . . as we feel the pull of who we truly are, on many, many levels.

Our new wings are fragile and damp, and we may feel reluctant to spread them at first, but we do; expanding our new, broad outlook, welcoming new people, and trying new projects.

The confident, enthusiastic joy-seeker in us is born and transformed from the juices of our old ways, creating us anew, sending us off with bright, sparkling wings, to fly from experience to experience, as we sample the sweet nectar of life, and as we give back by pollinating most of the life we touch, with love and connectivity.

Perhaps, through our metamorphosis, we change old behaviours, or we lose a few relationships; but we are energized, and at last we are the real person we are meant to be at this point in our lives.

As we step forward to help others during the various stages of their personal transformations, we consider the timing of our interactions with them; either stepping out of their way, or not disturbing them, or fluttering around and clapping our wings in harmony with theirs.

# Children Constantly Go through Mini-Metamorphoses

*'You see my two bright painted wings*
*as I go flying by.*
*I fold them when I land again*
*I am a . . . . . . . . . !'*


*Mrs. Browning, a grade two teacher, makes up various rhymes with a guessing word in the last line, and asks the class to quietly write down their answers. These are good lessons where she teaches her students to 1) stop, breathe, and think carefully about the clues given in each line, and 2) have the patience to not blurt out the answer right away.*


Children go through many mini-metamorphoses:

- There are times when they withdraw: *"I don't want to play with my friends today!"*
- There are times when they sulk: *"I don't know the answer. I don't care. I wish everyone would leave me alone!!"*
- And there are times when their transformation manifests in nightmares: *"There's a giant snake under my bed and it's trying to eat me!!!"*

We help children through their mini-metamorphoses, as the parent in us takes away any pressure and fear, and then once they transform, we help them to take all the knowledge they acquire during their chrysalis stage, and apply it to their new, fun, brightly-painted lives.

## *We Understand That We All Need Time for Daydreams*

Our brains are so skillful, as every day they switch back and forth between a third-person and a first-person perspective.

*They are resurfacing one of the lanes on the highway. The province needs it. That's great.*

*Okay, so the highway they're working on is the one I need to take to the city today, therefore I will have to leave half an hour earlier than planned, and if I'm still delayed, I will take the next turnoff and enjoy the scenic country roads where I can relax and reflect.*

We flick our third-first switch constantly in our daily lives, and then sometimes we keep our switch in the first-person position for a longer period of time as we do some reevaluating, adjusting, and planning of our lives.

Our night dreams, where our brains are free to wander where they please, reflect our reality as they try to make sense of it.

Our daydreams, however, are where we transcend beyond our reality and soar on the wings of hope, as we use our imagination to reevaluate and envision new possibilities, before we merge back onto our busy roads of life, with the knowledge that 'daydreams are our turbo-boosters.'

We are aware and respectful of others when they stop to take time to introspect – fixing any rough patches, cracks, or potholes – and we help wherever we can, so that they can drive off on a nice, new, resurfaced road; unhindered, and in full first-person control.

## *Our Solitude Is Our Charging Station*

As we walk along our beaches of time, we welcome periods of solitude when we can take in, and feel everything around us, as we reflect on the important role we play in the world.

~ *Sharon owns a car, but she rides on the train to work at an eye clinic in the city every day. During her daily train ride, Sharon sees the cows grazing in the fields, the gushing rivers, and the small, picturesque towns zipping by, as she reflects on her proud role of helping to make our beautiful world visible to all.*

~ *Rodney goes on a twenty-minute walk, twice a day, around the grassy perimeter of the grounds at the mill where he works. While he walks, Rodney hears the leaves crunching under his boots, the birds chirping, and the*

*machinery grinding, as he reflects on his*
*proud role of feeding the world.*

We are all conduits, allowing life-giving energy to pass
through us as we breathe . . . in . . . out . . . every now and
then holding our breath and plugging in to the powerhouse
of love, in order to recharge our true selves.

## *We Understand Time, Therefore We Are Patient*

*Mervin is passionate about playing golf, and his*
*friends love to play with him. They line him up on the*
*tee box and tee his ball. They hand him his driver. They*
*describe the terrain and distance of the fairway. Mervin*
*swings. They line him up again on the green. They hand*
*him his putter. Mervin putts. Mervin is blind.*

*One day, under a bright, cloudless sky, as Mervin*
*stands on the green after his drive from the tee box, his*
*friends place a strange stick in his hand. Mervin shakes*
*his head, "Wha–? What is this?"*

*Mervin suddenly feels himself being lifted into the air*
*to the sound of his friends shouting, "It's the flagpole,*
*Merv! Ace! Ace! Ace! You got a hole-in-one!"*

*Mervin's friends take away any of his insecurities*
*about the game of golf, showing him and themselves that*
*all things are possible when your heart is full of love and*
*your tour bag is full of patience.*

# Our Patience Is a Profitable Investment

From the moment we open our eyes in the morning, until the moment we close our eyes at night, we wait . . . for our coffee to brew, for our children to finish their homework, for our meals to cook, for our airplanes to land, for our paint to dry . . .

We are all patient, knowing that we make very wise investments in the assets of time:

- When we wait, we comprehend what is going on around us
- When we wait, we allow ourselves time to contemplate outcomes
- When we wait, we build up our confidence to act
- When we wait, we divide up our time for all those in need

As we observe our normal breathing patterns, we pause . . . we refrain . . . we think . . . we blink . . . and then, with a sigh, we step forward to take away the numerous roadblocks that we encounter on our journeys, or we help to take away the numerous roadblocks that others encounter on their journeys.

Our daily patience creates sound and lucrative long-term investments, which we all profit from in this lifetime.

# We Pay Attention to Each Other's Moods

*Lizbet, who is autistic, wakes up in a dark mood because on the day before her school trip to a farm is cancelled, due to bad weather.*

*Her personal assistant, Mr. Raycroft, collects a bunch of funny pictures of animals with sad faces, and during lunch he hands Lizbet a note with the pictures included, which reads, "Dear Liz, I know how disappointed you must feel because you couldn't see the animals yesterday, but this is what the animals felt. When we do go to the farm, once the weather improves, then we will have to check up on the animals to make sure they are all in better moods."*

*Lizbet chuckles, perks up, places a cookie in Mr. Raycroft's hand, and then goes on to enjoy the rest of her day.*

*Mr. Raycroft takes away Lizbet's sad mood about missing an event, by offering her a light-hearted perspective on her letdown.*

Our moods, little trip-ups on our path, disrupt our life rhythms, for example:

- Holes: where we do something that we need to dig our way out of
- Roots: where our memories are triggered by something that stirs within us
- Fallen branches: where we are hurt by something we see, or experience

- Mud puddles: where we are dirtied by something that we need to clean up
- Ladybugs: where we instantly deploy our wings in the celebration of victories

All these disruptions shake up the true and trusting regulator in our brain, which is in charge of our moods.

We love others through mood trip-ups by taking away any feelings of weakness, scars, pain, shame, etc., and if their rhythm is disrupted by a powerful, positive experience, we celebrate their mood with them while they are fueled by high spirits.

## *Why Is There an 'X' in Anxiety?*

*Zain is in bed with a bout of the flu. Prisha, his mother, keeps appearing at his door and asking questions about his health, and then when Zain answers, she follows up with another question, then another, and another.*

*"Ma, please, PLEASE! I've told you countless times, if there's something you need to know about my health then I will tell you." This ignites a question hurricane from Prisha. "Ma! Ma! Please stop!" Zain begs.*

*A little while later, Zain hears a voice in his head that says, "Ma is very worried about me, but sometimes 'talking' words just don't work."*

*The next morning, when Prisha brings Zain his break-*
*fast, Zain holds up a large piece of paper with the written*
*words: "Thank you, Ma. I am not feeling any worse today.*
*Please bring me more paper. I love you."*

*Prisha goes to open her mouth— and then she stops*
*and nods as a huge, gratifying smile spreads across her*
*face, followed by a little giggle.*

*Zain takes away Prisha's stress of needing to have*
*immediate, concrete feedback on how he is feeling almost*
*every hour, and the new form of communication between*
*them helps Prisha to relax, with the knowledge that she*
*will continue to be kept in the loop, without all the drama*
*attached. From that moment on, their 'talking' conversa-*
*tions are filled with positivity and fun.*

Why is there an 'x' in the word 'anxiety,' we ask? Is it
thrown in there to show us that anxiety is a roadblock that
we come across regularly, just like when we are driving,
and our engines start to shudder and grind, and our power
weakens?

When we notice that anxiety is stalling others, we offer
them reassurance by removing some of their nervous feelings, so that they can read signs, change gears, put their
foot down, and roar off in 'gaiety' after the 'x.'

## We Help Others When They Are Going Through a Depression

Depression throws us off course, and causes us to live between the lines of life as we travel through a long, dark tunnel. We know that beauty and love are all around, but we are unable to experience any of these things because of the enormous, solid arch structure encircling us, with walls so thick, so rigid, built to hold in all our strength.

Like trees in winter, outwardly we are not blossoming, but inwardly we are taking extremely protective measures to conserve our energy. In our dark tunnel, tired and weak, all we can see are the day-to-day routines that our headlights reveal to us.

The friend in us helps others through their dark tunnel of depression by removing feelings of helplessness and dejection, and by reminding them of their powerful abilities, as we embrace and cherish them.

And then, soon, towards the end of their tunnel, the light of the world appears, and as they blissfully navigate towards it, they begin to feel a sense of hope and belonging once again, as they get back 'on line' to live the true, explicit story of who they are.

## We Help Others When Their Bodies Break Down

*Melana is a student at a dance school, where she also teaches young students. One day she is involved in a terrifying skiing accident which leaves both of her legs paralyzed. Everyone at the dance school feels helpless, until a few months before they put on their annual concert for the students' families and friends, they ask Melana if she would like to participate, like she used to do before the accident.*

*Melana is thrilled, and a performance is quickly choreographed. The show begins, and one of the highlights is an outstanding dance of pirouettes and pliés encircling Melana's wheelchair as she gracefully displays beautiful upper body and arm movements. A few months later, Melana is once again teaching students, with the help of a highly talented demonstrator.*

*Everyone at the dance school helps to take away some of the feelings of inability which Melana may have felt, as they offer her hope; a powerful fuel that propels her to go on to have a successful career, to marry, and to mother two children— all from her wheelchair.*

We see these amazing, warm-hearted acts around us all the time. When bodies break down, others quickly step up to help remove some discomfort, using their tools of empathy, togetherness, and wholehearted love, so that we can all continue to dance together in the magnificent show called LIFE.

# Our Bodies Are Our Best Friends

*While two friends, Curtis and Harrison, are bodybuilding, they decide to give their bodies a name. The names they decide on are their actual middle names. "We can yell at James and Scott as much as we like," they laugh, "because they'll get motivated without getting offended. And at least we are also making use of all of our 'given' names."*

We travel together, our bodies and ourselves, as a great team of 'give and take.' We love how we breathe and how we vibrate, and how we communicate.

- When our organs slacken, we refuel them with wholesome foods and pure liquids
- When our muscles ache, we soothe them in warm water and essential oils
- When our brains misfire, we rid them of clutter and give them rest

- When we feel sick, our bodies rid us of toxic substances
- When we feel weak, our bodies strengthen our muscles
- When we feel overwhelmed, our bodies remind us of who we are

Our past sculptures us: freckles etched by the sun, creases carved by giggles and frowns, veins inflated by fortitude. We are 'one' with our bodies as we sustain, nurture, and expand them, in celebration of our sacred bond. We are a united team, we are eager, and we are caring, and strong.

Our relationships with our bodies help us to appreciate everyone's relationship with theirs, and wherever necessary to step in and take away any communication concerns that may hinder their endearing self/body relationship.

Our bodies are not just somebodies; they are our fleshy, faithful, very best friends, with great names.

## *We Help Others When They Are Tired*

*Ahmed is at home with his mother, supporting her through her illness. When his sister, Layla, arrives after a long journey, Ahmed tells her that he cannot understand why he is so tired because he only does little bits of work here and there in the home, while the rest of the time he sits around and keeps his mother company.*

*"I know why you are tired, my brother, because I feel the same way," says Layla.*

*"You do? How does this happen?" says Ahmed.*

*Layla embraces Ahmed and whispers in his ear, "We are emotionally tired, Ahmi. Worried about Mama, feeling her pain, concerned about her future. Our minds are drowning. We need to swim to the surface; all of us, together."*

*Layla and Ahmed begin a daily routine with their mother: strolls around the neighbourhood, eating highly nutritional meals together as a family, getting enough sleep, doing yoga and meditation, and writing down lots of wonderful memories in a large scrapbook.*

*After a while, Ahmed tells Layla, "I am now doing so much more, and yet I am no longer tired. I am motivated. I am energized. I believe my emotions are so focused on loving Mama now, that there's not much room left for those constant negative thoughts that keep pushing me down, down, down. I have risen to the surface, thanks to you, Lays, and now I can fully breathe again."*

*Layla embraces Ahmed. "I too have risen, Ahmi, and I believe I can feel Mama's alive and strong presence swimming right here beside us."*

The little babies of the world teach us to be very aware of their sleeping needs, and to know immediately when they are emotionally, mentally, or physically tired. This is when we step up quickly to give them the rest they need; anywhere, anytime.

Because of our experiences, when it comes to adults, we waste no time helping those who are very, very tired.

- When someone is emotionally exhausted, we help them to rest by taking away any feelings of loneliness and hopelessness
- When someone is mentally exhausted, we help them to rest by taking away any feelings of defeat and time restrictions
- When someone is physically exhausted, we help them to rest by taking away any feelings of powerlessness and pressure

Signs of tiredness are very strong, felt by ourselves, and also seen and sensed by others. This helps us to all work together in the world, as we rest, and as we encourage others to rest, so that we can all move sturdily along together, adjusting our sails and holding steady; remembering our little babies, sucking on their fists, and rocking their heads, side-to-side . . . hush . . . shh . . .

# WE ARE FORGIVING

Our happiness is not determined by promises kept, or forgiveness forthcoming.

Promises are plans and possibilities, backed by good intentions, which are made before we know, or we can foresee, any battering that we may take from life – from tiny trickling raindrops to heavy pounding hail – which make us pack up our picnic basket, roll up our blanket, and head back home.

Times can change, circumstances can change, and *we* can change; which means that what we pledge today may not be doable tomorrow. Our good intentions flow freely from our well-meaning, loving hearts.

## *Promises We Make to Ourselves*

*"I'm going to work on getting fit. I'm going to start a gratitude diary. I'm going to drink less coffee, meditate more, spend less, play more with the kids"* . . . the list goes on . . . and on.

## Why We May Not Keep Promises We Make to Ourselves

After making a promise to ourselves we can sometimes find that:

- We start procrastinating because we don't think we're good enough to honour it
- We feel overwhelmed by the commitment
- We run out of time
- We run out of physical or emotional energy
- We fear change; of routine, of surroundings, of status
- Our beliefs are in conflict and fighting each other, in our hearts and in our brains

. . . in other words, roadblocks suddenly appear on our road of life.

## Picking Up the Pieces of Broken Promises We Make to Ourselves

After breaking a promise we make to ourselves, we take a moment to re-examine our goals and hopes, along with our talents, intuitions, morals, and emotions; deciding where all our priorities lie at this precise moment in time.

This evaluation stirs up new positivity as we continue on our journey, all intact, after we have swept away all the broken shards on our road.

# Promises We Make to Others

*"I'll always be there for you. I'll drive you anywhere. It won't happen again. I'll bug you less, love you more"* . . . the list goes on . . .

## Why We May Not Keep Promises We Make to Others

There are a large number of reasons why we cannot fulfill our promises to others. These could be the same reasons why we break promises to ourselves, or it could be that our lives suddenly change and we are simply unable to honour the commitments we made.

## Picking Up the Pieces of Broken Promises We Make to Others

After breaking a promise we make to others, we take a moment to 1) find other ways of being there for them or 2) have faith that opportunities will arise, further down the road, when we'll be able to make up for what we were not able to do.

This reassurance stirs up new positivity for others as they continue on their own journey, all intact, after we have swept away all the broken shards on their road.

## Promises Others Make to Us

When people make a promise to us, they offer us a sign of trust that they will deliver on their word.

## Why Others May Not Keep Promises They Make to Us

There are a large number of reasons why others cannot fulfill their promises to us. These could be the same reasons why we break promises to ourselves, or why we break promises to others.

## Picking Up the Pieces of Broken Promises Made to Us

After others break a promise to us, we take away our expectations from them, while we lovingly let them know how their broken promise has affected us, and at the same time we get out of their way as we offer them understanding, freedom, and respect.

This understanding stirs up new positivity for others, and for ourselves, as we continue on our individual journeys, on roads smooth and clear, after all the broken shards have been swept away.

Because we are loving beings, we accept that things can change – our word, others' word – and although our weather can change unexpectedly, we don't change how we love, because we are the sun that continues to shine happily above the clouds.

## *What Sign Appears Most Frequently on the Road of Life? 'Forgive Yourself, and Then Quickly Move On.'*

*When Asha and her family immigrate from a tropical country to North America, they adopt a kitten, and name her Buttercup. Where they come from, because of the hot climate, all pets live outside the home, but now, in the colder climate, pets live inside, and this is when Asha's family is advised by many people to remove Buttercup's claws so that she doesn't damage the furniture.*

*After a veterinary surgeon removes Buttercup's claws, slowly and steadily a foreboding sense of guilt brews inside Asha, until one day she confesses her deep regret to a group of friends, "I have tortured and maimed this beautiful creature."*

*Asha's friends acknowledge how she must be feeling, while at the same time they point out how well Buttercup manages life, and how much Asha loves Buttercup, and also how very obvious it is that Buttercup loves Asha. Then one of her friends, Urbi, who works in an animal shelter says, "We did the same thing to our late cat, Jerry, when we arrived in this country many years ago, and I also felt, and still feel, the same way you do about it."*

*Asha scoops up Buttercup, cuddles her close, and then as she looks over at Urbi, a powerful feeling of under-*

*standing and forgiveness erupts in her heart; firstly for Urbi, and then, in her next deep breath, for herself.*

Because we understand that guilt can cause roadblocks on our journey through life, we remove all traces of remorse, and pay attention to all road signs relating to forgiveness, as our self-esteem perks up, strong and healthy, and purring loudly.

## Forgiving Others Comes Easy

Forgiveness is when both the forgiver and the forgiven rise up in their hot air balloons, high above the quagmire of emotions, to a quiet, serene place, where, surrounded by clean, healthy air, they are able to breathe with ease, filling their hearts with unwavering love and mercy.

When we are the forgiver, we are reminded of who we truly are, and how many hazards can appear on everyone's journey: the insecurities, the distresses, the mishaps, and the fears. Because of this deep knowing, we are able to forgive others for their actions, or inactions, with the understanding that everyone is at a different stage of their journey, at a different time.

When we are the forgiven, we are thankful that many hazards have been removed from our path, and we feel comforted, empowered, energized, and even guided, as we continue on our journey, all purified and beloved.

Even though we live in an ever-changing world, we continually allow good intentions to flow freely from our hearts, and when required, we courageously navigate our way through the cloudy periods of broken promises and pardons, which are then always followed by a new, golden, dawning of peace.

## *Peace Is a Gentle Trade Wind That Circulates Within, and Amongst Us*

We teach our children how to keep the gentle, peaceful wind swirling around and around continuously, by showing them how we all get out of each other's way in this world.

*"Riley, please keep your voice down in the store so that all the people can concentrate on their shopping."*

*"Greta, please keep Cheeky's cage clean, so that we can all enjoy playing with the cutest little hamster in town."*

Like our planet's tremendous trade winds, our peaceful dispositions are triggered at our equator – our core – and it is from this point within us that we breathe life into a powerful, peaceful movement that circulates the entire world, bringing enrichment and happiness to every life-form.

We build monuments for peace, we design safe homes for peace, we submerge ourselves in nature for peace, we forgive for peace, we solve conflicts internally and externally for the continuous airstream of peace. We *are* peace.

# WE EMBRACE AND SHARE OUR EXPERIENCES

## *We Help Each Other by Sharing Different Perspectives*

*Rodney and Hugh are in the pub having a good laugh about chicks and politics, and then, when Rodney asks Hugh where he was born and where he grew up, Hugh's jaw drops and his brows squeeze together as he replies, "Plymouth, 1940, and once, when I was a little kid, the sirens went off and my mum threw me into the empty bath and jumped on top of me until the cracks and thunder blasts passed. It was a kid's worst nightmare!"*

*Rodney's eyes open wide. "Wow! Incredible! You survived The Blitz!" he blurts out.*

*Hugh runs his hands slowly down his face, down his body, all the way to his knees, and then he leans over and pats Rodney on the shoulder and sighs, a long deep sigh, as if he is releasing a volcano of emotions before he says, "Rod, no one's ever reacted to that story like you just did. Everyone normally focuses on my fear and the trauma. So, you know what, I've always thought that was a horror story, but I'm now thinking, yes it was horrific, but more than that it is actually an incredible 'survival' story. I am a freakin' lucky guy, aren't I? Wow, next round's on me."*

*Rodney's powerful exclamation and response to Hugh shows that he acknowledges and understands the magni-*

*tude of horror little Hugh and his mum must have gone through, by contrasting it to the fact that he survived and then went on to live a meaningful, positive life. In other words, he takes away some of the darkness in Hugh's childhood memories as he taps into the winner in Hugh.*

## Different Perspectives Expand Our World

We all see things from who we are, and from where we are, at any given time; therefore we all have our own version of 'what is.'

Most of our conversations are filled with different perspectives:

- *"Oh no, it's raining." Or "Look at all the happy birds taking a shower to cool off."*
- *"Oh no, I gotta go grocery shopping." Or "I'm so glad that I have money, and that I'm physically able to push a shopping cart and purchase items."*

When climbers reach the summit of a mountain:

- The adventurer sees the breathtaking, grand, and impressive landscape
- The geologist sees the plateaus and peaks, and rock formations, sloping down, and up
- The mountain guide sees pride and gratitude on the climber's face

As we hike our way through our lives, others take away any narrow viewpoints we may have at certain times, by offering us a variety of perspectives that extend our field of vision, thereby expanding our world.

## We Gain a Helpful, Healthy Perspective on the Past, Present, and Future

If our perspectives become slightly constricted and we find ourselves intently focused on the past, to the point of feeling haunted by our experiences, we take a moment to consider how:

- The past has offered us an opportunity to learn
- The present now offers us time to put our lessons into action
- The future will offer us a rewarding experience based on our learnings

*"Just because my last employer fired me because of my lack of expertise for the job, it does not mean that I won't find another job where my expertise will be more than sufficient."*

If our perspectives become slightly constricted and we find ourselves intently focused on the present, to the point of being short-sighted about potential outcomes, we take a moment to consider how:

- The past has offered us an opportunity to understand that everything passes
- The present now offers us time to contemplate various outcomes before acting
- The future will offer us a rewarding experience based on our contemplations

*"Just because my health is currently perfect, it does not mean that I will continue to overburden my body with toxic substances."*

If our perspectives become slightly constricted and we find ourselves intently focused on the future, to the point of believing that we have full control of it, we take a moment to consider how:

- The past has offered us an opportunity to remember where life has led us
- The present now offers us time to only control whatever we can
- The future will offer us a rewarding experience based on our unassuming decisions

*"Just because our taxes will soon be hiked, it does not mean that I will stop donating to the animal shelter; even if it is a smaller amount."*

As we do with ourselves, we also help others when they are intently focused on just one period of their lives, by offering them various perspectives and time frames, which tilt their world back onto its normal axis, thus giving them clarity to navigate their journey, as well as a healthy balance to keep their wheels turning, and turning.

## *We Are Charitable and Humble*

*When Tiffany looks at her receipt after paying for her groceries, she smiles when she sees that she has saved ten pounds by collecting coupons, doing price comparisons, and redeeming shopping points.*

*Then, as Tiffany makes her way to her car in the parking lot, she notices a woman standing with a large sign that reads: 'I am a refugee with four children. Please, I need money to buy food.'*

*Tiffany loads her groceries into her car and then walks back to the woman and hands her ten pounds.*

*When Tiffany walks back to her car again, this time her smile is even broader than it was at the grocery checkout because, as she tells her husband later, "Receiving something is nothing compared to giving something."*

We are all generous, as the loving friend in us takes away deprivation from others, with the understanding that those who ask for help have a wonderful supporting cast of candidness, conviction, and confidence, which helps them find the courage and humility to speak their truths; and this, in turn, encourages us all to share our basic human needs with each other, which are generously supplied by our rich and bountiful planet.

# We Pull Aside Window Coverings to Behold the Beauty in All Things

From the viewports of a spaceship deep in space, to the scenic lookouts on the surface of our Earth, to the portholes of a submarine deep in the ocean, we are able to see, and feel, all the beauty of our glorious home.

*When Dave grows impatient at the long traffic light, Graham, who is sitting beside him says, "I love looking at all the beautiful, grubby car wheels when I'm stopped at an intersection. They tell an infinite story about our past, our brilliance, and our vision for the future."*

Beauty, in the form of sight, sound, or touch, ignites many centres of our brain, because it tells a story of the past, the present, and the future, as all three dimensions unite in a powerful burst of familiar, celebratory, and hopeful feelings.

The beauty of our skylines, rural and urban, tell mind-blowing stories of preservation and craftsmanship. The beauty of our bodies, inside and out, tell captivating stories of growth and achievement.

Everything on Earth, including colour, radiates beauty – instant stories that are seen, heard, and felt – which resonate with us all. The blueness of our sky and sea represents wisdom and devoted trust that when we help others by removing any coverings or fogginess they may have on their windows— their eyes, their ears, and their hearts are able to behold the beauty which expands their view, and opens volumes of novels, on their journey through life.

We love our existence, and where there is love, there is beauty.

## *We Are Authentic*

The more authenticity we show to the world, the more connected we become, because when we see the realness in others, we know that they will embrace our realness, as well.

*As Claire settles into the salon chair, she says to Cheri, her hair stylist, "I've seen that lady whose hair you just finished, a few times in the salon, and you do something different with her hair every time. Shame, poor lady, she can't seem to make up her mind about what she wants."*

*"Her name is Belisama, and she knows exactly what she wants," says Cheri. "She told me right up front that she wants to look different all the time. She's a great customer to have, business-wise, but more than that, she is a very open and forthright person. I love her company. There now, her honesty must be brushing off on me."*

We are not mirages – illusions of sunrises, wet puddles, and light pillars – we are all real; solid, genuine, and powerfully present.

We share our distinctive, true selves with everyone around us, as we scatter our authentic life seeds far and wide on fertile Mother Earth, which cultivate a magnificent life-force of true, unmistakable love.

Our walls – all the memories and ongoing experiences in our lives – are built around our great patience, our impartial perspectives, our unlimited kindness, and Earth's breathtaking beauty. With the use of all of our wonderful tools, we help each other through all the various stages and challenges we face, adjusting our frequencies to assimilate to the natural rhythm of life and the eternal power of true love, as we live our lives on our beautiful, breathtaking beaches of time . . . waves nuzzling up . . . hissing away . .

With our strong, unforgettable walls, magnificent houses are built, so that together, forever, we advance.

# PART THREE

# THE ROOF

The roof is the commitment piece of our relationships,
built to withstand the fiercest of storms.
No matter what, the roof remains secure,
sheltering and protecting the entire relationship design.

When Commitment speaks, it says, *"My pledge to you
is that I will trust you, I will remain loyal to you, and I
will protect you; and together, our gratitude will reinforce our dedication to a pleasing and plentiful world,
and together, forever, we will unify."*

## *Our Earth Is Committed, and So Are We*

Our Earth's roof – the atmosphere – is fully committed
to all living things, protecting us from heat and radiation,
while providing us with clean air, fresh water, sound waves,
and sunlight.

We humans are also fully committed to all living things,
as we open our hearts and minds to allow the universal balance of protection, air, water, sound waves, and sunlight,
to flow through us, and then to spread over everything and
everyone we meet on our journey through life.

Protection keeps our world safe; today, tomorrow, and always. Clean air fans our life force; allowing us to breathe, with love. Fresh water purifies us; promoting our growth. Sound waves carry our communication; connecting us all together. And sunlight warms us, lighting our way, day by day.

As long as there is commitment in our world and in ourselves, there is life.

## Our Commitment Is a Sequence of Trust, a Leap, and Loyalty

Life is a supreme cycle. Our trust evokes our leaps, our leaps evoke our loyalty, our loyalty evokes our trust.

## We Stand on Our Diving Boards of Trust

*As baby Sam takes his first few breaths and looks up at his mother, Trish, from within the worldly womb that now encircles them, he feels safe because he innately trusts that she is his lifeline.*

*A day later, Trish is moved to another ward to receive treatment for a postpartum complication. Sam then looks up at Juliet, the nurse who has him snuggled in closely and is feeding him from a bottle of warm milk, and he trusts that she is his lifeline.*

*Trish soon returns to the maternity ward, now healthy and strong. When Sam looks up at the two faces of Trish and Juliet, who both smile down at him within the worldly womb, his feelings of trust swell up to form an expanded awareness of security and love.*

We are born to trust. We trust every living and non-living thing within our biosphere, and far beyond. We know that it is through the very existence of our magical, expansive universe that we, individual humans, can exist. Our trust reaches beyond the stars. It is infinite.

Every day we stand poised at the end of our diving boards of trust, and then, when we are ready, we leap off into the beautiful, blue waters of loyalty.

We trust our bodies. We trust our minds. We trust all our social interactions that swirl around on our patriotic planet. Our trust is built on the knowledge that after we leap, if the waters below get rough, we have every tool we need at our disposal to survive. Plus, we have each other. We trust.

## *We Leap!*

- *Chatri and Sudha tighten their seat belts on the plane that's taking them to their new country*
- *Paul tightens his air tank valve and slips into the cold, murky lake to join the rescue team*
- *Cassandra tightens her microphone clip and runs out onto the stage*

## We Are Chain-Leapers

From large, life-changing events, like signing a new business contract or putting up a 'For Sale' sign on our lawn, to everyday doings, like trying a new herbal supplement or driving a new route, right down to the simple act of getting out of bed— we are perpetually taking leaps of faith. Leaping! Leaping! We are all chain-leapers!

## We Land in the Pure, Fresh Waters of Loyalty

Once we land in the water (try new things), we begin to expand (grow), and as we swim around, we feel at ease with our world, our minds, our bodies, and all those who leap and swim with us.

## Loyalty Promotes Trust; Trust Promotes Loyalty

In the pure, fresh waters of loyalty – where we commit to ourselves, to projects, and to others – our trust expands, which boosts our confidence, so that we can go back onto our diving boards and continue to take many, many more leaps of faith, into new, exciting, uncharted waters.

Through all our leaps of faith, we know that if ever things get a little rough – on our boards, as we leap, or during our time in the water – we will all be there to help each other; committed, loyal, and true.

We grow and thrive from the millions of leaps we take, keeping the cycle of life turning, by the trusting choices we make, in our nourishing, protective worldly womb.

## *We Are Dedicated, Inside and Out*

Our bodies are fully dedicated to keeping us focused and balanced, working constantly as they receive and process thousands of signals from our ears, eyes, muscles, and skin, to keep us stabilized on this great, orbiting, gravitational planet.

Because our bodies are so incredibly amazing at this task, we, too, are fully dedicated to keeping ourselves focused and balanced when it comes to living our lives.

We work constantly as we receive and process thousands of bits of information from our surroundings and from each other, so that we can navigate our way, and stay our course, as we live our great, devoted lives.

## *Our Commitment Keeps Us Motivated, Focused, and Centered*

*Micah's life dream is to work on an oil rig, like his father and his grandfather did. The only obstacle in Micah's way is sea sickness, however, he is determined to overcome his condition and make peace with the ocean.*

*He sets out on a course of balancing his body and*

*mind when they are swayed and tossed about. He works on his physical health through diet and decongestion. He works on his mental health through breath training, focus, and therapy.*

*Micah soon begins working for an oil company. After many long rides on offshore vessels, followed by long, grueling, and productive shifts on the rig, Micah leans on the high railing and stares out at the vast ocean wilderness, which surges and swirls all around him. He smiles. He feels steady and fully grounded. He is proud. He is content. He is at peace.*

Using all the tools we possess, the achiever in us is able to keep centered and focused on reaching our daily, and lifetime goals, as we dedicate time, energy, and knowledge into the process of achieving them.

Even though we are all challenged by new choices that circle our vessels every single day, we remain focused on our journey of love; forever positioning our sails and rudder, when we drift in the doldrums, cut through the calm waters, or when we toss in the turbulence.

We are dedicated to life. Because we *are* life.

## *We Are Reassuring*

Reassurance is the reinforcement of the roof, which keeps everything steady, and strong. To assure one another is to positively inform, and the 're' indicates doing it again, and again.

*Four-year-old Bryson cuddles up every night with his stuffed whale, Splash. As Bryson strokes, pats, and squeezes Splash, he relaxes with a little smile on his face, comforted with the knowledge that he is safe, and that everything is okay in the world.*

We all offer whales – which symbolise great communication – to each other. Our soothing strokes remove stress, our pats convey that we are all in agreement and that everything is fine, and our squeezes express our dedicated love for each other.

## We Are Committed to the Traditions That Ground and Bond Us

*A large group of friends meet every month at their local pub to enjoy a meal, a few drinks, and each other's company. When a worldwide pandemic hits, the pub closes in-door dining but still continues to operate on a take-out basis. On their regular pub nights the friends pick up the pub's take-out meals, connect on a Zoom meeting, and enjoy the food, a few drinks, and each other's cheerful company, from the sanctuary of their own homes.*

*The group of friends take away the forlorn feeling of loneliness from each other, and they also take away any feelings of instability regarding work from the staff at the pub, so that everyone can move on through life, always there for each other, for better or for worse; even when disrupting little intruders land on their paths.*

## Our Traditions Are Our Islands

From our rich, time-honoured cultural traditions, to our special family traditions, all the way down to our own personal private traditions, customary practices keep us all committed in love and in gratitude.

*Every Friday evening, after dinner, Aileen and Jack play music from the land of their birth. The songs and melodies stir up wonderful, nostalgic memories, which get their feet tapping and their voice boxes crooning, as they merrily toss away the stresses of the week.*

Traditions are the remote, magical islands we visit on our life journey through vast, open oceans, scattered with storms and shipwrecks, winds and waves. These islands are where we reflect, honour, pay tribute, and ground ourselves, as we watch all of our worries drift by.

Traditions – camping, celebrating the solstice, fruit picking, and many, many more – connect us to our roots, and reinforce our sense of belonging.

On our beautiful, sturdy islands of tradition, we take away insecurity and anxiety from ourselves and each other, as we provide consistency, structure, and safety, all the while reminding ourselves where we came from, where we are, and where we are headed.

Traditions reaffirm who we are
grounded and grateful
as we toss worries afar.

# WE ARE GRATEFUL

Using our imagination, talent, and commitment, we create a fantastically functioning world that houses us all in love and unity, and using our intellect, compassion, and commitment, we create an everlasting, lush paradise that houses all of nature in safety and strength.

We feel grateful for everything in our lives – from our morning stretches to our night dreams – and this gratifying feeling reaffirms that we are all part of this world, and that we had one in billions of chances of existing, and we won!

We are all winners; forever thankful to be a part of this life.

## Gratitude Is a Gift We Receive, Enjoy, and Then Regift

We are continuously receiving every requirement needed for a fair, fulfilled life: sustenance and shelter, aid and affection, pleasure and praise. We graciously accept, and apply all of these gifts to our lives, and then, without a moment's hesitation, we regift them to others so that they may feel the same impact of gratitude that we feel.

~ *Thank you, Grandpa, for all your brave actions during the war. That courage has been my pillar of strength through all the challenges I've faced as a defense lawyer.*

- *Thank you, son, for continually expressing your artistic talent. That passion has helped me to be open and receptive to all the high school art students I teach.*
- *Thank you, friend, for your love and support throughout my life. That goodwill has motivated me to do all kinds of fundraising work to help the homeless.*

We bake a delicious Black Forest cake with all the ingredients given to us from our generous planet. As we shovel each spongy, tender morsel into our mouths, while our tongues worm around our lips to scoop up a juicy, sugary cherry, our tastebuds dance in celebration of the scrumptious, chocolatey delight. Then, as we look around the table at the people who we are sharing our cake with, our enjoyment immediately doubles.

Receiving anything in our lives is the overture of our joy; regifting it is the grand finale.

## *Our 'Thank Yous' Shake Up the World*

The word 'thank' is a thought, a gesture, a gratification, and the 'you' points to others who give us gifts which we truly appreciate; from opening a door for us, to helping us study or heal, to attending our conferences or donating to our cause. We thank you.

There are variations of 'thank yous' all over our world, but fundamentally the gentle 'thank you' gesture unites us all. Like a snow globe, our world is in constant 'shake-up' with all our thank yous floating gracefully around like sparkling, pure sapphires.

We are eternally thankful for everyone's participation in our lives: our family's, our friend's, our country's, the world's. Thank you. Thank you. Thank you. Thank you.

## *Our Compliments Echo on and on*

*Joan: "I like your dress."*
*Tammy: "It's nice of you to say that."*
*Joan: "It's kind of you to say I'm nice."*
*Tammy: "It's sweet of you to say I'm kind."*

Our compliments echo on and on, leaving a wonderful, mood-lifting afterglow in their wake. The frequent exchange of compliments boosts moods and makes everyone feel appreciated for their appearances and achievements, as we are all reminded of who we truly are . . . are . . . are . .

## *We Consume Food with Gratitude and Reverence*

Children love to hand out food to others: snacks to guests, pizza slices to classmates, treats to puppies, and seeds to birds. The delight on children's faces when they pass food around expresses the awareness that we are all programmed to share our basic human needs, for the sake of our joy and survival.

All the food we eat was once alive – plants and animals – then it reincarnates after we eat it, to become our own flesh and blood, for which we are eternally grateful. As our bodies receive food – like a squirrel who just unearthed a nut, or a seagull who just found a French fry – our bodies rejoice on a very deep level.

We appreciate every mouthful of food we eat, not as a substance, but as a 'life upcycled to give us life.'

## *We Consume Food Together to Celebrate Life Begetting Life*

*Every day Theo, Ema, and their four children sit together around their blackwood table enjoying wholesome, delicious meals, but as the children approach their teenage years they come up with more and more excuses to grab their plates and eat in their bedrooms.*

*When a fire destroys a nearby house, leaving both parents deceased, Theo and Ema adopt their only child, Tommy.*

*It isn't long before Theo and Ema's children are back at the table, every day, embracing Tommy, offering him seconds, and making him feel like he is part of the family.*

*When Tommy grows up, Theo and Ema's children – using their business, real estate, and logistics qualifications and knowledge – help Tommy open up, and run a homeless shelter and soup kitchen, where he often joins those he's feeding in the dining hall filled with blackwood tables.*

*Tommy helps Theo and Ema's children to reunite at mealtimes, and Theo and Ema help Tommy by taking away the prospect of isolation as they eat together in a setting where the power of life-giving food is distributed amongst them.*

As it is with the growth rings in a tree trunk, the time of a forest fire shows a deep, dark scar, followed by circles and circles of wide-spaced rings which indicate an easy period of sunlight, air, moisture, and nutrients.

Food gives us life; consuming it together with others gives us linkage to life.

# WE ARE DEVOTED TO KEEPING OURSELVES, AND OUR PLANET, FULLY FUNCTIONAL

*When the guests leave Daniel and Lola's wedding they are each given a little spruce tree sapling as a memento. The story of this lovely couple will undoubtedly be remembered for generations to come, as the trees grow up to nourish the planet, to house wildlife, to provide shelter, and to purify the air that we breathe.*

We are perpetually organizing, decluttering, recycling, and cleaning everything around us, as well as everything within us, pausing every now and then to take in the magnificence of our efforts.

## *Our Earth Organizes, We Organize, and Together We Blossom*

Earth is organized: The rotation, the moon cycles, the water cycles, the seasons, and so on.

We are organized: Our brains are high-grade, well-regulated processors that assimilate and store information (images, events, memories) and then release results based on new, earth-shattering ideas that enable us to run our lives by a routine of giving and receiving, and setting goals and reaching them, all in consistent harmony with our Planet Earth.

*Cindy is a human resource manager for a large, lucrative company which no one has resigned from, or has been fired from, in three years. The owners of the company put a lot of this down to Cindy's great organizational skills, including her ability to help staff members organize their own lives around their jobs, if and when any roadblocks appear on their paths.*

From personal day planners to retirement strategies, from grocery shopping to home-cooked meals, from parenting young children to sending them off to university or to live on their own, we all set priorities, arrange everything around them, and then prepare for a beautiful tomorrow.

We will never be fired from this large, lucrative planet, because we are all organized.

## *We Declutter*

Our brains are great minimalists that like to get rid of irritating thoughts that nag at us:

- *"There's lots you have to do."*
- *"What about your past mistakes?"*
- *"What will others think?"*

Such reflections make us stop, reflect, and then shuffle all the clutter away.

We are constantly decluttering our homes, our lives, and our planet, clearing the way for new progress.

*Skylar does temp work, with the hope that it will one day lead to full-time employment. One day he starts a temp job at a property development company where he is asked to sort out and rearrange a storage area crammed with files.*

*After weeks of sorting, shredding, filing, and labelling, Skylar reduces all the paperwork and files by half, and he is immediately offered full-time employment as an Office Assistant, and it is not long afterwards that, amongst many other transformations in the office, the once messy, disorganized kitchenette in the back looks like a cozy, upscale espresso bar.*

Decluttering is the step we take before we recycle, as we clear away areas to create space where new developments can brew.

## *We Recycle*

Our brains are great recycling plants that gather waste – worn out, damaged, or infected scraps – and then send it on to be generated into new, reusable, good energy.

*Curtis, who sits on the town's committee board with developers and environmentalists, has a great idea for an old estate home situated on many acres of property in the middle of the town. "The word that comes to mind whenever I'm at a meeting about developing this site, is 'recycle,'" he says.*

*A year and a half later, Curtis and his family stroll around the estate, now called Rixon Park, amongst beautiful canopies of healthy original trees still left standing, as well as comfortable picnic benches, sturdy tables, colourful playgrounds, and beautifully crafted gazebos and stages, all built from the older, decaying trees that were cut down and repurposed on the property. All around people are picnicking and frolicking as they enjoy the magnificent harvest of the 'recycling' seeds that were planted at the town meetings.*

We are all driven recyclers. We observe things, sum up their value, determine what they would mean to others, and to our Earth, and then we act, moving things around to land in places where they are most useful: charity shops, food kitchens, animal shelters, textile recycling plants, and many more.

Recycling equals evolution, as we reclaim, reconstruct, and repurpose all the wonderful material we have on our Earth.

# We Clean

Our brains are conscientious cleaners that are constantly mopping up unnecessary debris to be carried away in an infallible, antiseptic fuel.

*Mila creeps forward into the drive-through car wash, and as her wheels click and align onto the tracks, blobs of soap rain down on the roof . . . and onto Mila's head, lap, and steering wheel! She has left her sunroof open!*

*While she reaches for the switch to close it, water sprays into the car, and then suddenly everything stops, and the attendant comes bouncing along to her window.*

*A little while later, Mila stands and laughs in the reception area after cleaning up – using lots of towels which the staff have given her – and as she reaches into her purse to pay, the girl behind the counter raises her hand and says, "Sorry, the instructions for the car wash are very explicit. We only wash four-wheel vehicles, and because in your case, you exposed your steering wheel too, making it five wheels, there will be no charge for you today."*

We are all constant cleaners. From the little blow of our noses, to housecleaning, to hospital sterilization, to massive environmental clean-ups . . . we clean, clean, clean . . . making space for new growth and nourishment, while always making sure that we rest enough so that our brains can clean themselves.

And then with a new, restored, fresh brain, we remain forever ready with soap and a pail to do our bit in the world of cleaning, and in some cases, overcleaning.

Everything on Earth is here for a reason, and when we clean we shift material from one place to another so that we can all function, fully and efficiently.

We all help each other to clean;
our lives, our windows, our lakes and springs,
our cars, our roads,
and thousands and thousands of other things.

We are all great organizers, declutterers, recyclers, and cleaners, which makes our world the phenomenally successful business that it is.

## We Keep Each Other Safe

From the beginning of time, our ancestors have done everything they can to keep us all safe. And now, we do everything we can to keep ourselves and our future generations safe. The indestructible acts of safety prevent all the destructible acts which we may encounter on our journeys.

All the warning signs that we pass on our road of life are there to keep us safe:

- STOP: *Abigail says, "I am a quality controller, STOPPING and inspecting all items before they are shipped to market, where excellence is paramount in keeping consumers safe."*

- SLIPPERY ROAD: *Dominic says, "I am a firefighter, averting us from SLIPPING into blazing tragedies, where focus is paramount in keeping everyone and everything safe."*

- SPEED LIMIT: *Vivienne says, "I am a financial adviser, preventing us from SPEEDING into economic hardships or bankruptcies, where prevention is paramount in keeping all clients financially safe."*

- ANIMAL AND HUMAN CROSSING: *Nicolas says, "I am an alarm system designer, alerting us to potential COLLISIONS with unforeseen events, where pre-warning is paramount in keeping our world safe."*

As we stand on our diving boards, ready to take great leaps of faith, again and again, the safety we all offer each other promotes our overall trust, and ultimately diminishes the number of obstacles that can land on our paths.

We are all deeply committed
to keeping each other from hurt
from the tiniest raindrop
to the mightiest cloudburst.

Our organizational skills – in our brains, in our bodies,
and in ourselves – help us to generate many more moments
of mesmerizing walks on our beaches of time.

# WE ARE COMMITTED TO CARE

## *Busyness Does Not Get in the Way of Our Commitments*

*Makena's friends keep inviting her to different events – a hike, a festival, a bazaar – but Makena simply doesn't have the time in her busy home life to accept most of the invites. Makena isn't one to tell any type of lie in the form of excuses, etc., and she also thinks that if she tells her friends she is too busy, they might feel unworthy of her time.*

*So, instead, Makena tells her friends that she will somehow make time for them, and she does. She loves writing poetry, so she decides that whenever she is waiting for a meal to cook, a child to waken, or a load of laundry to dry, she will write a poem about her friends. The poems and haikus turn out to be set amongst trees and birds, cheering and feasting crowds, and merchants and colourful crafts.*

*Makena presents all of the poems to her friends on plates of homemade Moroccan shortbread cookies, and tells them, "If my plates are going to be full, let some of them be full of my love for you."*

*Makena's friends treasure the gesture, their poems, and their adoring Makena for decades to come.*

*Makena is not going to allow 'time' to rob her of love. She takes away any doubt her friends may have about her trust and loyalty, and her open honesty; and her friends do the same for her.*

It is a busy world, and we are honest about our jam-packed lives, which can sometimes lead to interesting ways of staying together, forever joined by the lyrical love in our hearts.

## *Our Committed Healers Heal on Many Levels*

*As Charlie lay on the chiropractic drop-table, getting adjustments for his lower back strain, in a gentle, calming voice, Dr. Fletcher, knowing that this kind of back strain is ultimately treatable, says, "Charlie, think about the countless number of times your body has healed, ever since you were a kid; from fractures, inflammation, scrapes, diseases, muscle disorders, and so on. We all have more healing mechanisms in our bodies than we can ever imagine."*

*After the appointment, as Charlie walks out of the clinic into the parking lot, the trees appear greener, the flowers brighter, the bird's song sweeter, and his back feels relaxed and stronger.*

*In Charlie's case, not only does Dr. Fletcher ease open joints so that they can release nerve irritability in his spine; he also takes away nagging, negative thoughts in the prefrontal cortex in Charlie's brain, creating space for new perspectives and optimism.*

Our healers are attentive to the various levels of our suffering – our bodies, our minds, and our inner-selves – and they treat them all with empathy and expertise, clearing away obstacles so that we can journey on, aligned and at ease.

## We Volunteer Because We Are All Beneficiaries of Human Kindness

Volunteering flows through our veins, and like our blood, which carries life-giving oxygen around our bodies to nourish us and to fight off infections, we do the same for others; from helping a stranger carry their groceries or conducting traffic during a power failure, to helping in a hospital or cleaning animals in an oil spill, to supporting children's education worldwide or delivering supplies to disaster zones.

The child, parent, and friend in us
is always ready to volunteer
which turns the wheels of the world around
pumping powerful, pure love into every sphere.

# We Go the Extra Mile

~ *Sharon volunteers as a caregiver. When she visits a client she takes along various scented oil samples, and then once the client chooses a sample that appeals to their senses, Sharon adds a few drops to their bath water and suggests that they relax in it for fifteen minutes before she bathes them.*

~ *A town's annual five-kilometer walkathon for Learning Disabilities is cancelled because of major flooding where the event normally takes place. However, the organization's volunteers decide to walk, and raise money anyway. Some of them form small groups and walk five kilometers around their neighbourhoods, while others walk alone, in their own time, wherever and whenever they can.*
*Their story catches the eye of a local businessman who, with a huge donation, matches, and far exceeds the amount of funds that were raised the year before. "No amount of water is going to wash away the care that our volunteers so lovingly give to our community," the businessman comments.*

We know what is needed for ourselves, and for others, and when we are in a position to give, there are no boundaries, as we take a deep breath and we walk that extra mile, in sunshine or in rain.

# *We Care for Our Caregivers*

We care. And because we do, we care for those who care for others, as we offer them respite – a time away – from the ongoing tasks of caregiving.

Our caregivers know what to do for the person they are caring for:

- They help them to retreat for a while from what ails them.
- They engage in conversations and activities with them, reflecting on their life, and life in general, so that they continue to feel connected to everyone and everything.
- They make sure that they are comfortable in their surroundings so that they feel relaxed.
- They offer them healthy sustenance for their bodies, and their minds, so that they feel rejuvenated.

When we offer our caregivers some respite care – where they are free from the responsibilities of caregiving for a while – they are able to do for themselves what they do for others, as they utilize our gifted time by retreating, reflecting, relaxing, and rejuvenating, before returning to the ongoing tasks of caregiving.

Caregiving is a wonderful, healthy balance of giving care and receiving care, so that we can all catch our breath— and then increase our care.

## Our Reward for Volunteering Is That Doors Are Opened for Everyone

*Alfred is a mail carrier in a large city, and after he passes away in his eightieth year, his wife, Esmeralda, reveals the following: "Alfred would pay close attention to the families he delivered mail to, and when he saw that a family was struggling, he would slip some money into their mailbox. He never needed anyone to know about, or thank him for, his generous gestures; his thanks was simply in the form of knowing that he was helping others in some small way."*

We don't expect accolades for our volunteering because we simply do what we were born to do: slip priceless letters of love into everyone's mailbox.

## Our Cups Remain Full

In our world, everything begins with us. We do not pour from an empty cup.

*The volunteers at the hospice smile at forty-six-year-old Charlotte as she serves apple cider to clients and tends to their comfort – a cushion propped, a crocheted blanket spread, a tissue passed, a rummage for a pair of dropped eyeglasses, reassuring words offered after a test result – week after week, month after month. And Charlotte knows the right words to say at the right time, because she understands the clients, and she feels their pain.*
*"That must be very difficult."*

*"So sorry to hear this."*

*"I am always here for you."*

*It's a Tuesday evening when all the hospice volunteers gather for their monthly meeting. The volunteer coordinator stands, and opens her binder. The room quietens. "Before we begin," she says, "I'm so sorry to tell you that we lost a very dear client on Saturday after a three-year battle with cancer. A severe setback led to complications and kidney failure . . ."*

*This type of announcement is part and parcel of the work at hospice, but it's never easy for the volunteers to hear. "A beautiful soul, Charlotte Amanda Paton!"*

*The volunteers gasp, and cry softly. Sorrow spills over, fusing them all together in a ruby light as they feel Charlotte's presence in the room with them; comforting them, and whispering the right words in their ears, "I am always here for you."*

*Charlotte's mission in life was to give back, every day, in every way, for all the days of her life. Even though she had a terminal diagnosis, Charlotte's cup was filled with love and compassion as she helped to take away obstacles from the lives of others who were with her in palliative care.*

Our help towards others is always forthcoming, even as we accept help ourselves. The loving friend in us never grows weak, as long as we continue to breathe . . . in . . . out . . .

# WE ARE COMMITTED TO OUR SENIORS

We respect our Seniors – the great pioneers
of free thought and free speech –
who roared into battlefields of war, weather,
inhumanities, and diseases,
seeking solutions and victories along the way;
never stopping until they succeeded.

## *Beauty Bursts Forth as We Age*

When we look in the mirror in our later years, the reflection of who we truly are becomes more and more focused as we see our ancestors nod, our baby smile, our child laugh, our teenager wink, our young adult place a hand over their heart, and our parent, traveller, artist, collector, achiever, joy-seeker, winner, dreamer, and friend in us, all give us a thumbs-up to indicate that we are doing great.

The more we age, as we look around us, the more beauty we perceive, because we see countless stories in everything we come into contact with.

> *When Ingrid sees a bunch of Oxeye daisies, she sees her grandmother's garden, colourful tasty salads, bridal bouquets, healing*

*ointments, and herself skipping along sunny, wide-open plains.*

- *When Manuel sees a horseshoe-shaped arch, he sees his village church, operas at the international auditorium, bridges, and himself riding his pony around a green, grassy paddock.*

- *When Luis sees a waterplane in the sky, he sees his favourite birthday gift, beautiful boats, family celebrations, eagles, and himself transporting hundreds of people to the canyon.*

When we look at our Seniors we see all of these reflections in their faces too, images that tell countless stories; stories that we need and stories that we enjoy, as well as stories that inspire us to reach new, great heights.

## Our Seniors' Stories Offer Us a Roadmap on Our Journey

When we listen to our Seniors' stories, we create a rewarding and constructive way to spend time with them, we help them to reunite their families, and we help them to feel part of something bigger and more meaningful than their everyday life.

- When we hear our Seniors' stories of survival, we know that we will always overcome.
- When we hear our Seniors' stories of heroism, we know that we will always succeed.

When we hear our Seniors' stories of love, we know that we will forever be supported and cherished by one another.

We are very dedicated to our Seniors, removing any debris in their way, so that their roads remain smooth, wide, and scenic, as we stand by our pledge of protection and devout loyalty.

## We Help Our Seniors If Their Windows Become Foggy

Just as our Seniors consistently wipe away any fogginess on our windows, we do the same for them. Love has no age boundaries because, as long as we live, we breathe, as we take, and give.

*Elsa's eighty-second birthday is fifteen days away. From a young age Elsa is a seamstress, a craft which she gives up years before because, in her words to her granddaughter, "Nel, I've tried to get along with robots, but every time someone pushes me to use a modern sewing machine I can't stitch a straight line, I can't sew thick fabric, and there's a movie screen on the thing which you have to keep touching. Tarnation! I miss my good ol' friend, the Singer. Well, I suppose I'm just an old geezer now who can't do much anyhow."*

*Nel hugs Elsa tightly and goes off to make a plan. The next day she visits Elsa, hands her a small box with four-*

*teen cards inside, and says, "Granny, starting tomorrow, every day please take just one card out of the box from the top and read it."*

*Elsa follows Nel's instructions, and every day she feels more and more empowered. Why? Because each card tells a short story about a person over eighty years old who has, and in some cases still is, achieving remarkable things: running marathons, skydiving, entertaining, cooking for the masses, and so on.*

*Then, surrounded by her family on the day of her birthday, Elsa pulls the last card out of the box and reads it out loud: "Your old friend is back to help you thread the eye, pump the bar, guide the cloth, and come out a star." With that Nel places a large, wrapped box in front of Elsa, who rips it open to find an old Singer sewing machine, in perfect condition.*

*Nel takes away any insecurities Elsa has about her abilities, and with that Elsa goes on to spend many years sewing beautiful items for all the family. The gift from Nel brings the family even closer together, as the fabric of their unit is symbolically stitched together in a priceless, heritage quilt.*

We are devoted to keeping our Seniors' windows sparkling clean; one steady, meaningful, stitch at a time.

# WE REMAIN LOYAL TO EACH OTHER, IN LIFE, AND IN DEATH

The expression 'Loved One' refers to everything and everyone on our beloved Earth, because we all exist based on our breath of removing obstacles and expressing love.

The death of a Loved One throws a large, immovable rock onto our path; something that causes us to veer off the road for a period of time before we are able to return, restored.

From a baby in our womb or in our arms, to a long-lived centenarian, during our grief we gaze around at all the empty spaces that are no longer filled with our Loved One's large, powerful presence, where they once connected with us; within us, in our home, in our community, in our country, and in the world.

Like snowflakes, we all experience our grief in our own way, in our own time, while we are exposed to a wide range of elements encircling us. This means that we all have different needs at different times, as we drift wearily through the turbulence of loss.

## Grief Is More than One Loss

When a death occurs, those left behind can suffer many tiers of losses: a home, financial security, relationship identity (husband, mother, etc.), role as a caregiver, life purpose, self-confidence, faith, friends, family, community, hope, goals and dreams . . . and one of the most difficult losses suffered is the loss of a Loved One's memories as they slowly begin to fade.

These losses amount to many hazards on our journey through the rough country; like harsh terrain (a feeling of utter helplessness), darkness (a feeling of forsaken loneliness), and violent weather (a feeling of distressing hopelessness). However, nothing can drown out the comforting, reassuring voices we hear in the background, from the same people who will help us to enshrine the beautiful memories of our Loved One.

## *We Reach out to Each Other in Times of Grief*

Our love for each other is magnified during the grieving process, as we reach, reach, reach, far into the hearts of others, to comfort them, to help them, and to reassure them that we are always there for them, walking beside them on the shifting sands of time.

The death of someone close to us leaves us with a feeling of deep despair, where denial, disarray, and desolate loneliness often emerges.

- When others are in a place of denial during their grief, Mother Nature is protecting them, only allowing small amounts of awareness to

surface here and there, so that they can handle their overwhelming emotions slowly . . . steadily . . . step by step . . .
This is when we remove the pressure of time from others, and we are very soothing, calming, and patient with them, accepting and respecting that time will heal all, in its own time.

~ When others are in a place of disarray during their grief, they may feel confused, rattled, battered, and overwhelmed, lost in a stormy sea, as past, present, and future emotions toss them about.
This is when we remove some of the confusion from others as we say and do things that offer them clarity and stability, throwing them a lifeline so that they can float along and focus on signalling lighthouses and guiding stars, which gently steer them as they mourn.

~ When others are in a place of loneliness during their grief, they may feel mournful and numb, with no passion, purpose, or desire to participate in anything without their Loved One.
This is when we remove any feelings of disconnectedness from others through our actions and our words, which reassures them that everyone is there for them, and that they are loved and cherished, the same way that they loved and cherished their Loved One.

# We Are Unified and Strengthened in Grief

Our unification with one another is magnified during our grieving process, a unity that is felt in every corner of our interconnected, compassionate planet. From majestic elephants who congregate to bury their dead, to whales who amass and scream mournfully when one of them washes up onto the shore, to birds who gather and cover their dead with twigs, to rodents who assemble to sniff and lick the bodies of their lifeless mates . . . we collectively feel, and mourn all loss.

A loss, no matter how small, jolts the natural rhythm of our planet that moves in perfect harmony with the universe. If we see a dead rabbit on the road, we feel a jolt of sorrow for the poor animal, and we also feel a jolt of sorrow for our world.

For warmth and protection, many species, like blue-birds and small fish, huddle together. This is also what we humans do as we gather together to form a solid bond, especially during grief, which strengthens us, protects us, and saves us from despairing loneliness.

*Melody, a bereavement group facilitator, suggests that each of the eight attendees in the group write down an affirmation, which is like a little piece of debris in a stormy ocean that they can hold onto as they drift along, until they eventually see the shore. They write:*

- *I will be patient, and journey through this for as long as it takes.*
- *You are my hero; I am now going to try to be yours.*
- *I have enough power to keep moving on.*
- *The clouds overhead will pass – they always do – and the sun will shine on me again.*
- *You are showing me how much I can love.*
- *I will look out for you in everything beautiful I see.*
- *Your work will never be done, for I will continue to do it.*
- *You built up my world to weather the Great Storm of Death.*

*Towards the end of the session, the attendees ask if they can share their affirmations with everyone in the group. After they read their affirmations out loud, paper, pens, and scissors are quickly brought into the room, and after a lot of writing and cutting everyone leaves the group session with eight thought-provoking affirmations, which they can regularly recite to keep them connected to their Loved One, and also to remind them of where their strength lies.*

We are committed to each other – in life, and in death – embracing each other through every storm, and with our undying love we help each other to return to our roads of life, which gradually become illuminated under bright, glowing rainbows.

## We Remember, and Honour Our Loved Ones

Just as it is during our initial grief, we also go on to remember and honour our Loved Ones in our own way, and in our own time.

## We Talk to Our Loved Ones

*James has a photograph of his late wife, Mary, pinned to the corner of his easel, and as he dips his brush to begin a painting, he gives Mary a little nod and blows her a kiss. After his painting is complete, James thanks Mary for her inspiration through the love they share, which will live on forever in his heart.*

We are always touched when someone speaks to their Loved One at a funeral: *"You will be sorely missed,"* and so on; so something on a deep level tells us that this human behaviour of speaking to those who have passed on, is very natural.

## We Feel Our Loved Ones

*The Paquet family continues to place a setting for their late grandmother, Adeline, at every Christmas dinner, which they all cook from hand-written recipes in Adeline's recipe book. Before the family begins eating, each person explains where they feel Adeline's presence:*

- *"In the children's laughter."*
- *"In the candle's glow."*
- *"In the symphony of carols softly playing in the background."*

Our Loved Ones live on as we are united by them, and as we are inspired by them.

## *We Visit Our Loved Ones*

As Rosemary places a poem upon her mother's grave, the clouds burst open and the sun beams brightly down onto the land.

### *MOM*
*You gave me life*
*You showed me light-heartedness*
*while you demonstrated unconditional love.*
*You taught me fairness*
*as you grounded my beliefs.*
*You exercised kindness, always.*
*My world is brighter because of you.*
*Like water and steam, although*
*we exist in different forms,*
*together we are timeless.*

We all have sacred places where we visit our Loved Ones; from national memorials, to local graveyards, to commemorative items cherished in our own homes.

- *When Niall lights a candle cupped by a stone angel, every year on his late mother's birthday, he feels her strength and her radiance.*
- *When Cynthia places fresh flowers on her husband's grave every month, she feels his beauty and his perfection.*
- *When Liam enters his office and glances at his sister's teaching certificate on the wall, he feels the power of all the great things she achieved in her lifetime.*
- *When Kenji sits on a bench engraved with his father's name, he feels Papa's presence next to him, and the comforting feeling that he will never be alone.*

Our hearts are always open to receiving wonderful memories of our Loved Ones, and rejoicing in the powerful impact they had, and continue to have, on our beautiful world.

Whether we have lived alongside someone for a long, or short period, or whether we have not even met them in person, we are grateful for their trust, their courage, and their loyalty, which keeps our world inhabited with devoted, loving beings. Our commitment to our Loved Ones never ever dies. It is timeless . . .

Our commitment to Earth, and to each other, is built under the strong canopy of trust, loyalty, and protection, where we share food, love our seniors, and where we help each other to heal from loss. We remain eternally thankful and committed to taking trillions of leaps of faith which keep us all safe and happy. We are dedicated to love, and to life.

With our secure, sheltering roofs, magnificent houses are built, so that together, forever, we unify.

# PART FOUR

# THE DÉCOR

The décor consists of all the merriment, the games,
and the shenanigans in our relationships,
that keep us liking each other, that keep us human,
that keep our feet planted firmly on the ground.

When Décor speaks, it says, *"I decorate your life with smiles, hugs, playfulness, entertainment, sport, and a bold, adventurous spirit to travel to happy places filled with warmth and wonder, and together, forever we will rejoice.*

## *We Speak Volumes with Our Hugs and Smiles*

Hugs tell heartwarming stories of togetherness, devotion, and love; and smiles are the story titles.

HUGS: As we reach out our arms to embrace someone, our heart chakras align and open, allowing empathy, compassion, gratitude and pure love to flow freely between us, in a powerful swirling whirlwind filled with every positive element that exists in the world.

Holding someone close draws all life into the moment; a moment when every word spoken is demonstrated by a powerful, meaningful action.

Greeting hugs, consoling hugs, triumphant hugs, affectionate hugs, group hugs, farewell hugs . . . our hugs reaffirm that we are always there to support, and love each other, through every chapter of our snuggly, interconnected lives.

SMILES: When we smile, the muscles surrounding our mouth and our eyes flex, saying: *"I speak kind words to you."* and *"We see how wonderful you are."*
Smiles represent many story titles:

- *'Welcome to my world'*
- *'I want to get to know you'*
- *'Everything is going to be okay'*
- *'You are amazing'*
- *'I like you'*
- *'We are unified'*
- *'I will miss you,'* . . . to name a few.

Smiles welcome us to a beaming world of words:

- A child's smile is a story of innocence and great expectations.
- A teenager's smile is a story of confidence and great courage.
- An adult's smile is a story of gratitude and great achievement.

Our hugs and our smiles unite our world in the Solar System's largest book fair.

# WE DECORATE

## *We Decorate Each Other's Lives*

*It is mid-December, and, as the plane approaches the shoreline after flying over the vast Atlantic Ocean, the captain makes an announcement: "Ladies and Gentlemen, we will be dimming the cabin lights for a while, as we draw our attention away from the constellation of shimmering stars that we've witnessed across the galaxy, to the constellation of shimmering Christmas lights below, that reflect our unity."*

*Everyone's eyes widen as the dazzling display comes into view, and it is not long before the cabin is filled with cheerful chatter, which continues on for the rest of the flight.*

Our planet is decorated with oceans and lakes and extraordinary aquatic creatures, with trees and flowers and amazing land animals, with canyons and volcanoes and beautiful birds, and with us. And because we appreciate our natural surroundings so much, using our talents and creativity, we work diligently to preserve it, enhance it, and replicate it, so that we can all live in a constant state of awe and wonder.

## Our Decorations String Us Together

Our lives are basically spectacular; however, decorations are a far-flung, colourful net that gathers us all together to celebrate, share, and showcase our lives, and everything we have, here on Earth.

- Our decorations honour our memories – from jewellery engraved with names and quotes, to museums filled with relics and stone – as we take away feelings of finality from each other, so that beautiful memories can live on.

- Our decorations honour our present day – from flowers delivered to our front door, to glorious festivals of colour and light – as we take away feelings of gloom from each other, so that we can be filled with delight.

- Our decorations honour our future dreams – from Valentine's Day cards sent with a promise of love, to new island resorts on the beach – as we take away feelings of lament from each other, so that together our dreams can be reached.

All our decorations are replicas of our natural world: The shapes: leaf and animal ear triangles, honeycomb hexagons, sunflower circles, and starfish stars. The lights: glow worms, sunlight, moonlight, and fireflies. Plus all the wonderful colours that radiate from everything on our world, and beyond.

Our net scoops up all the beauty on our generous planet, in celebration of its splendour; and, if needed, our decorations also shine a bright light on others' shadows, if they are in a time of healing.

The sensational artists in all of us are mesmerized by Earth's loveliness, as we express our exultation through decorations gathered in our colourful nets.

## *We Are All Dedicated Collectors*

Our collections (inanimate or functioning) keep us motivated, committed, and proud; from tinseled teaspoons, to precious friends, to useful knowledge, to valuable artifacts in our world's finest galleries.

When we collect, we are self-motivated. *Simon is a model train collector who travels the continent to research, purchase, and refurbish old locomotives, which he displays and operates in hand-crafted landscapes for everyone to see.*

When we collect, we are committed. *During the summer, autumn, and winter months, Whitney collects large amounts of second-hand clothing from her town residents, and then, every spring she holds a huge, low-cost rummage sale in the town square, for those in need.*

When we collect, we are proud. *Andre studies book after book about addictions, gathering a vast collection of knowledge on the subject, and then, when he helps people to kick their addiction habits, he is proud, the recovered are proud, and the world is proud.*

We collect for ourselves. We collect for others. We bring our collections to life; and vice-versa.

We decorate and collect
to showcase our time spent here
and to get us all chattering
about our divine earthly sphere.

# WE PLAY

Wheels, and drills, and mighty windmills, all move towards a central point. Our 'play' on the planet is the same centripetal force that:

- Tosses away tension and raises our joy
- Kicks away chaos and raises our composure
- Nudges away naivety and raises our awareness
- Smacks away solitude and raises our connection with each other

We make little bets to add amusement, we sing while we harvest, we have fun with shop assistants, we add humour to meetings, and we all dance when we get the chance.

Our globe is a great, glorious merry-go-round, with all its creatures smiling and laughing, merrily, merrily, as they hold on tight and spin around and around.

We are all born ready to play, day by day, for the rest of our lives.

## *Our Play Is a Display of Happiness*

Play is an impulsive action sparked by explosive emotions of joy that shout, *"WE ARE HERE! TODAY! TOGETHER!"*

*Every morning in class, Miss Mickelberry writes one letter from the alphabet on the board, followed by an action, which she encourages her students to perform.*

- ~ **B**ounce a ball. Watch how Earth will always play with you. Watch how Earth throws the ball back up at you, and how it never gets tired of the game.
- ~ **D**ance with Earth. Earth's dance is called Weather. Stamp your feet with the rain. Shudder with the thunder. Swoop and spin with the wind.
- ~ **J**ump. Feel how Earth will not let you get away. Feel how Earth wants you to stay right here. Feel how important you are.

Animals have fun chasing and tumbling as they express joy for their families, their groups, and their habitat. Humans have fun mimicking animal movements – flying like birds, diving like fish, leaping like kangaroos, and running like gazelles – along with all the other exciting things we do that keep us laughing and cheering together, as we express our joy for everyone and everything.

When others' lives become a little entangled, we reach over and help to untie any knots, with gestures of playfulness and fun; here, today, together.

# Playgrounds Transport Us Beyond the Rides

*Dawn invites Ava, a new immigrant, to her favorite amusement park in the city, called Fantasy Fortress. The large structure is made up of ladders, slides, silver tassels, a long green tunnel, bridges, and colorful ball pits.*

*As the two girls climb up the structure, Ava tells Dawn about her favourite amusement park called Vulture's Crown, in the mountains near her village. As the two girls look down from the highest platform in the structure, Ava says, "We are at the summit of the Crown. Let's climb down to the pond below."*

*Ava and Dawn climb down the steep rock face and run along the zig-zagging path where silver grass dances around them. They enter the forest and hop onto a fallen tree lying across the river, and then they both jump into the colorful, bubbly water with a loud splash!*

*After they finish playing, Ava and Dawn both turn to each other and say, "Thanks for taking me to your favourite amusement park."*

Indoor playgrounds and outdoor playgrounds – manufactured and natural – transport us all to faraway places where the joy-seeker in us takes our imaginations along for the ride.

# Our Teasing Is Playful and Bonding

*Bobby and his friends are getting bored as they hang out in the city park, waiting for the nearby stadium gates to open before a rugby game.*

*Don, one of the friends, says, "Hey, why don't we do some laughing yoga?"*

*Everyone nods in agreement. "Okay, so let's breathe in deeply, and as we exhale let's meditate on Bobby's laugh, which sounds like a tipsy kookaburra that's eaten too many fermented berries."*

*Everyone takes a breath, and as they exhale Bobby starts laughing, with a low hiccup-like cackle, and then he tilts his head back and expels a screechy, squawky, side-splitting racket from his belly. The others join in, and the harder they laugh, the harder Bobby laughs, until everyone is rolling around on the ground, with necks jerking, shoulders shaking, and arms waving.*

*After a while, the stadium gates open. Bobby and his friends scramble to their feet. Bobby presses his palms together against his heart and says, "I am eternally grateful for that yoga session where we huddled together in a good, gyrating scrum, which felt like a great party that didn't leave me with a horrendous hangover."*

Animals tease each other – a little peck here, a wild chase there – and little kids enjoy a good tease of peek-a-boo or *"Look here, kiddo, mom's drinking your juice,"* which says that we all see each other, that we all like each other, and that we all care about each other.

Through playfulness and laughter
we help build self-esteem
as we open others' pressure valves
so they can release excess steam.

As we ride on our glorious merry-go-rounds, up and down, and rotating around, the movement jiggles all the joy we feel in our lives, and spews it out with our bright smiles and kookaburra laughter.

## We Keep Life Lighthearted for Ourselves and for Others

Just as natural light benefits our health and well-being, our 'making light' of various situations helps us to achieve goals, to maintain our natural rhythms, and to feel happy and hopeful.

*Frank and Maria are watching their budget and cannot afford to take their children out for supper to their favourite restaurant, like they used to sometimes do, so they decide to replicate the restaurant in their own home.*

*They cook the meal which the children usually order, they put up a sign in their dining room with the restaurant's name on it, and they set the table with lots of cutlery and cloth napkins. They put on aprons, and, acting like wait staff, they serve the children their food.*

*"Here you go, young man. Enjoy your meal."*

*"Is everything to your liking, young lady?"*

*After that, every day when the family sits down to dinner, the children joke around, continuing to act as though they are in a restaurant. "Excuse me, excuse me, ma'am, sir, would you please top up my water?"*

We try not to burden our children with adult anxieties, but instead we show them how lightheartedness lessens the burdens we bear, especially when it comes time to paying the bills.

## We Perform in Shows to Showcase All of Our Stories

*Sanura takes her niece, Louise, to see an animated movie about a little lost warthog who eventually finds a home with a family of porcupines. "I know what that little warthog went through," Sanura tells her niece after the show, "because when I was a child I was all alone, and I eventually found a home with a family who did not speak my language, but who took good care of me, and loved me anyway."*

Dramas, comedies, horrors, and wild adventures, all tell a story of something we can relate to as our emotions are aroused; causing us to cheer, laugh, squirm, or flatten our quills.

A screen and a stage are huge doors into a world of remarkable stories of who we were, who we are, and what we have the potential to be: found, and at home, in the now.

# We Compete to Remind Ourselves of Who We Are

*Manning wants to improve his body strength before he begins work as an arborist. He does some bench-pressing and weight-lifting alone at home, and then after a while he decides to join a gym.*

*When he sees other men lifting heavier weights than he has been using, Manning pushes himself even harder, eventually tackling many more physical challenges than he thought he was capable of. Soon Manning is climbing trees with the strength and agility of – what he calls – 'a Manning Mandrill Monkey.'*

*When Manning surrounds himself with competition he:*

- *exposes himself to possibilities*
- *pushes his own limits*
- *reminds himself of his own inner strength*

Every day we compete with the person we were yesterday, improving our talents as we cook a better curry, write a better staff report, build a better cabinet . . . getting better and better with every action.

Competing with each other draws the same benefits as competing with ourselves, as the achiever in us practices patience, improves performance, and pushes limits towards another one of the trillions of prize trophies that sit, shimmering, right within our reach.

# We Keep Focused on Knowledge and Know-How

*Shawn has a history test coming up. "Try not to be too nervous, Shawn," his father tells him.*

*Shawn responds, "I'm okay, Dad. I try not to think about competing for A's and B's, or how well I'll do, but instead I try to focus on the actual history stuff; like how fascinating it is how the Romans built the revolutionary aqueduct systems back in ancient times."*

*Ironically, when Shawn graduates from school, with all A's, he goes on to become an engineer, working on a major project for a large city's waterfront.*

When we take tests, or write tests, we understand that, on our journey through life, tests are pit stops, where we pause to stop a leak, by placing a plug into the pond of skills and knowledge which we have acquired up to this point.

## We Play Sport to Separate Us, So That We Can Unite

When we applaud, we separate our hands in order to clap them together. Sport involves rounds and rounds of applause.

WE SEPARATE: In every sport – individual, partners, or team – we separate, and begin training and strategizing, all the while keeping track of our progress.

With wide open hands, our coaches, who, in some cases, are ourselves, push us to a place of possibilities; working out ways for us to advance and win, and taking away any doubts and discord, until we are ready to play the sport.

WE CLAP: After starting with a hard clap of passion, we all go through a dual of back-and-forth emotions:

*"We're nervous."*
*"We can do this."*
*"What was that?"*
*"Phew, that was close."*
*"What's going on?"*
*"We've got this."*
*"Oh no, we're losing."*
*"Oh yes, we're winning!"*

However our emotions 'play' out, like a great football player who holds onto the ball, the winner in us handles it all.

- *When Marilyn loses a game of tennis, she congratulates her opponent, and then she congratulates herself for eventually mastering her backhand.*
- *When Gianni loses a motor race, he congratulates the podium winners, and then he congratulates himself for breaking his own speed record.*

From tossing scrunched-up papers into a wastebasket in a quiet office, to thumb-wrestling for the last roast potato at dinnertime, to hurtling towards the goalpost in a crowd-packed stadium— sport unites us all; as we train, as we compete, and as we celebrate our glorious victories. *Clap! Clap! Clap!*

## *We Celebrate Each Other*

*Andrew and Jay stare at the old dial-up telephone in their local museum, wondering how to use it. After the curator shows them how to stick their finger in the hole by the number they want, and then turn it clockwise until it stops at the little metal barrier, they both go home, research, and do an entire project on the history of phones – going back to the original box telephone – and this gets both Andrew and Jay a good grade in science.*

*We celebrate our hard-working innovative inventors, who in turn celebrate us.*

Our celebration of each other is done in many ways:

- OUR PAST: We build great monuments, we maintain well-stocked museums, we polish victory medals, and we march in unison; to remember all those long gone, so that they may always live on.

- OUR PRESENT: We share triumphant stories, we present distinguished awards, we observe special dates in time, and we donate to mighty causes; to celebrate each other's success, so it can spread afar, and impress.
- OUR FUTURE: What lies ahead will be built from all the stepping stones of celebrations in our past and present day; based on all the remarkable things we have done, and continue to do, in every way.

As we all prance around on our planet, we are always looking for opportunities to lift each other up – higher, higher – celebrating like we do with this book, with voices ringing out, loud and clear: *"We honour you! We've got you! We love you!"*

## We Celebrate All Birthdays Which Transform Our World

A huge ripple effect occurs when we are born. Family dynamics change, which leads to community dynamics changing, which leads to country dynamics changing, which leads to our world dynamics changing. We embrace the celebration of all birthdays, which offer us an opportunity to give thanks for knowing others, to acknowledge their importance, and to reassure them that we will always walk beside them, now and forevermore.

Birthdays are monumentally significant, after all, the moment we enter the world, we disturb everything on a planet that will never, ever, be the same again . . . ripple . . . ripple . . .

## We Give Gifts with Layer Upon Layer of Wrapping

The gifts we give to one another have layer upon layer of wrapping, which says:

- *"We are celebrating your existence."*
- *"We are endorsing the things which make you happy."*
- *"We are honouring your relationship with us."*
- *"We are uniting us all by sharing the wonderful talents we possess."*

Gifts boost us up to a great vantage point, where we can get a magnificent view of the colourful, nonstop parade, on our very merry planet.

# WE APPRECIATE AND CELEBRATE EARTH

As we all move around on our planet, we are always looking for opportunities to take everything in, from every angle, through countless lenses.

When children draw pictures of their homes, they generally frame the structure with trees and flowers, and a bright yellow sun. Children's lenses may be small, but their peripheral awareness is widespread, as they wallow in the comfort and beauty of all their surroundings.

Because we are all a part of Earth:

- When we see a flock of birds, we feel trustful and hopeful
- When we smell a blossoming flower, we feel rooted and happy
- When we hear the sound of water, we feel nourished and cleansed
- When we feel the sun on our face, we are rejuvenated and motivated to bask in the glory of this life, in this place

We all feel 'at home' on our comfy, cushy planet where we rest, and play, and grow day by day, and where we are filled with eternal gratitude for our time here, our unity here, and all the senses we possess to enjoy the here, and now, under a bright yellow sun as the child in us lives on.

## *We Travel to Connect with Others*

*Nina belongs to a charity organization which travels to a country where there is a shortage of eyeglasses. Nina and the team stay at a pleasant hotel in a town where they are made to feel very welcome. "This place feels like home," Nina says in a text to her husband back in her homeland.*

*Each day, the team treks through the mountainous countryside to conduct basic eye-exams, and to hand out donated eyeglasses to a large number of villagers, who in turn share wonderful life stories, hugs and kisses, and delicious chunks of homemade smoked cheese and marinated mushrooms, as a 'thank you' to the organization, which, to them, symbolises a magnificent lighthouse. "This place truly, truly, feels like home," Nina texts again.*

Our hearts beat bravely as we hop off our nests and flap our wings faster, faster – up, down, up, down – as we soar and glide into a neighbouring town, or a national province, or a faraway country.

Like the Earth's glowing atmosphere, travel stories have many layers. We travel for various reasons: to relax, to volunteer, to explore, to shop, to find ourselves, to learn, to get a break, or we simply travel for travel's sake.

We all live in different parts of our widespread world, and the desire to travel draws us towards each other; to meet, to learn, and to share.

As all our senses are ignited in our travels – the sights, sounds, scents, and feelings – the adventurous traveller in us knows that deep down, even though we do not reside in these places, any feelings of seclusion are removed, because all the places we visit are another room in our home; therefore they *are* our home.

We are always on hand to take away any obstacles that stand in the way of us all enjoying our life of smiles and playfulness, competitions and sports, entertainment and celebrations, and the priceless gift of free movement around our bright and decorative planet.

With our warm and wonderful décor, magnificent houses are built, so that together, forever, we rejoice.

# IN THE END, WE HAVE ALL LIVED IN EVERY PART OF OUR HOUSE

Our world and our lives work together in perfect synchronicity of taking and giving. The world's snow and greenery retract and extend, retract and extend, creating a perfect environment for us to exist in. And we breathe in and out, in and out, creating perfect relationships as we move, stop, take, move, stop, give thanks . . . all in the name of true love.

We are valiant beings, equipped with a bountiful, bottomless bag of tools, and as we travel on our own unique journeys through life, we know that we all matter, every day, in every way.

The solid base of our relationships – built from integrity, empathy, and interactions – moves us passionately, meaningfully, and caressingly through our lives, as we help and respect one another, so that together, forever, we flourish.

Our respect starts with romantic partners, children, and siblings, and extends to everyone on Earth, in equal amounts. We take pride in knowing that we are here, today, upholding the far-reaching, life-preserving quality called dignity.

The memories and experiences of our relationships – built from an understanding that life is forever-changing – moves us patiently and calmly through our lives, as we wait and support one another, so that together, forever, we advance.

We accept each other's moods and unkept promises, and we stand by each other through body breakdowns and tiredness. We take pride in knowing that we are here, today, upholding the authentic, insightful quality called patience.

The commitment of our relationships – built from loyalty, security, and gratitude – moves us gracefully and confidently through our lives, as we honour and thank one another, so that together, forever, we unify.

We devote time and effort to traditions, and we help others who are suffering or who are less fortunate than ourselves. We take pride in knowing that we are here, today, upholding the trusting, unwavering quality called devotion.

The décor of our relationships – built from the light-heartedness all around – moves us contentedly and happily through our lives, as we play with, and entertain one another, so that together, forever, we rejoice.

We come together for fun, games, travel, and adventures, and we help others to cheer themselves on. We take pride in knowing that we are here, today, upholding the uplifting, pleasing quality called merriment.

All four parts of our house reflect the solid, adventurous, committed, lighthearted love which we all hold deep within our hearts, as we continue to remove obstacles in order to **L**et **O**thers **V**enture **E**asily, and as we continue to celebrate our great lives on our glorious planet.

# IF WE WERE TO DIE TOMORROW

If we were to die tomorrow
we need not confess
that in the House of Earth we lived
in the basement where we always felt safe,
only letting in an occasional, suitable visitor,
never daring to venture upstairs to open windows
should we be burned by sun, drenched by showers,
or ruffled by breezes.

If we were to die tomorrow
we can all proclaim
that in the House of Earth we
lived in every room,
always climbing the stairways so that

we could lean out of windows
where we felt the warmth of sun, the cleansing of rain,
and the exhilaration of cool breezes.

We explored our house every day
and we kept the doors and windows wide open
for all people and creatures to enter, as we welcomed them.
We have stroked the ocean floor!
We have kissed the clouds!
We have embraced the whole planet!
Although in the end our life was only a small beach
in the eternal sands of time—
we claimed that sunny shoreline and held on to it firmly
It was ours! It was ours!

*All of Us*

# LIST OF TOPICS IN SIGH

# About the Author

Lesley Marcovich has always drawn out the true essence of who we all are and how we all love, with her broad perspective on life through:

1. witnessing and experiencing personal life-changing events, e.g. unnatural deaths including suicides, developmental disabilities, immigrations, etc. plus a wide variety of celebratory milestones

2. conducting reminiscing groups in retirement homes and doing bereavement counseling and group facilitating for hospices, where she helps others to remove many obstacles on their journey through life

3. ghostwriting, where she helps others to step onto the centre stage of authorship

Lesley currently lives in Newmarket, Ontario, with her husband Bruce, in a home with a huge symbolic revolving door that enables all family members to enter, to remain, and to leave, in harmony with their life journey.

Visit www.lesleymarcovich.com to continue to remember who we all are, as we pump powerful, pure love into every sphere of our spectacular planet.

44516980R00116